"Dr. Ofosu integrates knowledge from years of study, professional thriving and lived experience into her work. The relevance of her book cannot be timelier. She brings heart, brains, and guts to her book and makes me proud of my profession."

Dr. Tatijana Busic, *Ph.D., C.Psych., Clinical and Organizational Psychologist*

"This is the book we've been waiting for! Dr. Ofosu has a deeper understanding and wider breadth than most of her peers. She unfurls sensitive and complex issues, integrating them into a digestible and progressive manner to guide employers and employees."

Esther Schvan, *M.A., Career Development and Transition Coach*

"As a former executive, I see tremendous value in this book if/ when employees hit rough patches at work. This will also be a great toolkit for leaders and HR professionals who aspire to be more modern and inclusive."

Tina Walter, *M.A., Diversity, Equity, and Inclusion Consultant*

"This is a valuable resource for employees working in organizations where problematic and traumatizing behaviours are rampant. Clinicians who help clients cope with these situations and their fallout will also appreciate this book."

Kafui Sawyer, *Registered Psychotherapist, Trauma Consultant, Founder and Executive Director of Joy Health and Research Centre*

"Dr. Ofosu explores important yet overlooked career issues and addresses 'the elephant in the boardroom' highlighting the challenges that racialized communities face in their careers. She provides thoughtful and practical information to help people avoid or bounce back from career-related adversity."

Dr. Janet Mantler, *Associate Professor, Organizational Psychology, Carleton University, Ottawa, Canada*

T0373537

HOW TO BE RESILIENT IN YOUR CAREER

This book shares vital career advice to help professionals navigate common "internally disruptive" career experiences such as harassment and bullying, imposter syndrome, membership in an underrepresented group, toxic workplaces, discrimination, and more.

Dr. Helen Ofosu draws on 20 years of helping employers acquire talent and coaching professionals through difficult career choices to unpack these layered and complicated issues in an easy-to-follow way. Dealing with the dark side of management, the book outlines various issues that can occur in the workplace, or during a person's career journey, and offers practical advice on how to overcome these obstacles and setbacks. Using her considerable HR experience, Dr. Ofosu also offers coveted insights from the employer's point of view. For people who have already tried other options to resolve their complicated career issues, this book offers an essential guide that equips readers with a knowledge base to make informed decisions around building and sustaining a thriving and resilient career.

How to Be Resilient in Your Career: Facing Up to Barriers at Work is a reliable resource presented with nuance, depth, and specificity. Psychologists, psychotherapists, social workers, and HR professionals who are looking for effective advice when supporting people struggling with these issues, will greatly benefit from this book, as will early career professionals and established earners looking to resolve their career issues.

Dr. Helen Ofosu is an Organizational Psychologist who offers Coaching, HR Consulting and Training/Public Speaking through I/O Advisory Services Inc., Canada. She is also an Adjunct Professor of Psychology at Carleton University, Ottawa, Canada.

HOW TO BE RESILIENT IN YOUR CAREER

FACING UP TO BARRIERS AT WORK

Helen Ofosu

Routledge
Taylor & Francis Group

NEW YORK AND LONDON

Designed cover image: © Getty Images

First published 2023
by Routledge
605 Third Avenue, New York, NY 10158

and by Routledge
4 Park Square, Milton Park, Abingdon, Oxon, OX14 4RN

Routledge is an imprint of the Taylor & Francis Group, an informa business

Library of Congress Cataloging-in-Publication Data
Names: Ofosu, Helen, author.
Title: How to be resilient in your career : facing up to barriers at work /
Helen Ofosu.
Description: First Edition. | New York, NY : Routledge, 2023. |
Includes bibliographical references and index. |
Identifiers: LCCN 2022036659 (print) | LCCN 2022036660 (ebook) |
ISBN 9781032358178 (paperback) | ISBN 9781032358529 (hardback) |
ISBN 9781003328988 (ebook)
Subjects: LCSH: Career development–Psychological aspects. |
Psychology, Industrial. | Self-help techniques.
Classification: LCC HF5381 .O46 2023 (print) | LCC HF5381 (ebook) |
DDC 650.1–dc23/eng/20220805
LC record available at https://lccn.loc.gov/2022036659
LC ebook record available at https://lccn.loc.gov/2022036660

ISBN: 978-1-032-35852-9 (hbk)
ISBN: 978-1-032-35817-8 (pbk)
ISBN: 978-1-003-32898-8 (ebk)

DOI: 10.4324/9781003328988

Typeset in Palatina and Scala Sans
by KnowledgeWorks Global Ltd.

Access the Companion Website here: www.theresilientcareer.com

This book is dedicated to the people who have been encouraging and supportive about the book – and the work that it is based on. In 2012, when I announced my plan to start a coaching and consulting practice based on my foundation in Psychology, some people looked at me a little sideways. But, from day one, my partner Errol, my brother Kofi, and my parents agreed with my belief that it was the best way forward. My son Kojo was similarly and consistently encouraging, cooperative, and supportive.

Years ago, my sister-in-law Lori innocently said, "You should have a blog, everyone else has one, and you have so much to say ..." I'm glad I listened because, without the experience of ongoing blogging, this book would probably have seemed too daunting. My long-time friend Amber gave me valuable advice about writing relatable and engaging material and using social media for professional outreach. All that informal writing served as essential practice that made this book possible.

I also dedicate this book to clients whom I've supported (and who have supported me) over the years.

Contents

Acknowledgments

I'd like to acknowledge the efforts and support that I've received from Todd Hunter who helped me frame this book and guided me from the initial concept through to the point of reaching out to potential publishers.

Melissa Hiller, Stephanie Regan, and Lewis Kavanagh have worked with me over the years to help keep my blog and newsletter alive. All of those efforts were important milestones and made for tremendous practice before this project came together.

Jay Schwab and Tim Fry have been there since the beginning of I/O Advisory Services to make sure that my hardware, custom software, and other technical infrastructure were in place. Doug Minter, I will always be grateful for your introduction to Malaika Adero who in turn, connected me to Todd Hunter. Gideon Oti-Gyamfi, I appreciate your diligence and support when it came to compiling the references and endnotes. Finally, I thank the clients who have trusted me with their hard problems that forced me to dig deep and co-create solutions.

Introduction

Years ago, I was earning a respectable income in a stable job, but I didn't think that I'd be able to last another 20+ years within that environment until I would be eligible for retirement. I had friendly colleagues, good benefits, a solid pension plan, and plenty of paid holidays – but I was bored. No amount of coffee was enough for me to power through a typical workday.

I am grateful that during that time I was able to work with an experienced coach to help me identify some options. He was wise and helpful, though I wish I'd had more in common with him. The fact that we were so different made me wonder whether he understood enough about my circumstances to be able to offer the advice I needed. He led a different life than I was living, had retired from an executive position, and had followed a very different career path than mine. He was quite a bit older than I was, so when he started his career, he didn't need much formal education to be successful. I, on the other hand, had started my career with a PhD in Work and Business Psychology (officially known as Industrial and Organizational (I/O) Psychology, a branch of Applied Social Psychology) and I'd been recruited straight out of graduate school. I was in a highly specialized niche at work.

When I started my career, I noticed that, aside from my colleagues, very few people had ever heard of my branch of psychology. I often found myself explaining that the "industrial" side of my work concerns itself with matching people to work roles where they are likely to perform well, whereas the "organizational" side of my work is about how organizations affect individual people's behavior – organizational structures, management styles, social norms, etc.

are all factors that influence how people behave within an organization. It's certainly not as widely known as Clinical Psychology, which helps people with their anxiety, depression, trauma, and other personal challenges. My niche made me a real subject matter expert rather than more of a generalist leader like the coach.

Career mobility was complicated for me because there were a limited number of promotions possible in my vertical niche. I started my career working for the Canadian federal government, a huge organization that currently employs about 300,000 people. I was hired as a personnel psychologist which wasn't a role that existed in most departments, and therefore it was not a "portable" role. If I had been an economist or a policy analyst, it would have been easier to move around to almost any other federal department. In principle, I could have searched for a more generic role and made a lateral move that could have led to the government's version of the C-Suite, but my background really didn't look like other executives' backgrounds. This is not to say that I lacked leadership qualities or potential, it's only that I did not fit the classic template. Even more, it would have felt strange to set aside all that I had learned in graduate school to find a completely different type of role so soon after graduating. My coach and I were both in Ottawa, Canada. At the time, Ottawa was not known for its diversity so it's not surprising that he was white. As a white man, his experience in the workforce and the types of challenges that he had faced were quite different than mine as a professional Black woman. The fact that I was also a working, divorced single mother with a young child made our realities even more divergent.

Still, we accomplished a lot as coach and student. But it was through our work that I realized that there were several non-traditional ways that I could use my skills and abilities. I went on to find a different role that was satisfying … until it wasn't. Little did I know that, years later, I'd be supporting others through their own career transitions and leadership challenges.

For over 20 years, I have helped hiring managers and employers clarify what they're looking for in future hires and then developing reliable and valid ways to identify job candidates who meet those criteria during a hiring process. Often this meant specifying the skills, knowledge, and abilities (i.e., the hard skills) and measuring them carefully. More importantly, this often also meant specifying the soft skills, namely, how someone will apply their skills, knowledge, and abilities.

In so many professional roles these soft skills determine who will be a high performer at work. Intuitively, we all appreciate that not all lawyers, surgeons, mechanics, or dentists are created equal – despite their similar credentials, technical skills, or knowledge. What separates these professionals is how they apply their expertise to create optimal outcomes for their clients. Despite this tacit awareness, too few employers spend enough time evaluating these soft skills when they are making hiring or promotion decisions.

The insights that I gained when creating hiring processes and the "assessment tools" (e.g., screening criteria, screening tests, structured interview questions and scoring criteria, simulations, role plays, situational judgement tests, and assessment centers, etc.) are useful when I am helping clients prepare to participate in competitive hiring or promotion processes. Since I've also designed assessment tools that were used to determine who was admitted into various leadership development programs, I also understand the essentials around career development, mentorship, and succession planning.

Someone generously said to me, "you've got the wisdom of a credible Work and Business psychologist who bridges the gap between employees' ambitions and employers' expectations." I thought her characterization of what I do was spot on.

I have learned a great deal as an HR Consultant working closely with leaders and other professionals to solve various problems. My background, however, is different from classic HR people. Sometimes my perspective is broader than HR, especially when I am looking beyond one HR transaction (e.g., one hiring decision or resolving one interpersonal conflict) with a view on the bigger implications on corporate culture, leadership, and inclusion. Other times my frame of reference is more granular and specific than a traditional HR perspective such as when I am identifying observable behaviors closely aligned with the soft skills essential to a particular role – and creating a way to assess those behaviors during a hiring or promotion process.

Occasionally I've gotten perplexed looks from people when I explain what I do for a living. Someone might ask why would high-earning professionals need career coaching? Well, some advice that I got when my son was a toddler seems apt: Little children have little problems, and bigger/ older children have bigger problems. It's the same for working professionals, business owners, and executives. People with impactful, wide-ranging mandates and high salaries often have more complicated work-related and leadership issues. They also want to get their advice from someone who understands the nuanced challenges that they are dealing with. Even people who are closer to the beginning of their career can encounter resistance and fail to launch, although they have the potential to become successful. The metaphor of planes taking off into the wind is powerful – and strangely relevant. The idea is that despite a ton of resistance, the plane still takes off.

Sometimes, during a successful person's career, they face too many challenges at once and it can feel impossible to marshal the energy to do what is necessary to push through. Starting new jobs, launching major projects, advancing while managing heavy parenting responsibilities, or making any meaningful change often feels difficult to navigate. It can feel like a bumpy road, or it can be as unsettling as violent turbulence. It is as though there are hidden obstacles and pressures that keep pushing, making it harder to accomplish goals. The gravity and inertia of how hard this can be keeps many people down and unable to find the means to take off in their professional lives and in other important endeavors. In part, *How to Be Resilient in Your Career: Facing Up to Barriers at Work* was written to make it easier to push past difficult circumstances by putting credible information and strategies in one place and making them accessible. As noted by an anonymous reviewer of this manuscript, this book also deals with the dark side of management – the many interpersonal, structural, and societal factors that create bias and mistreatment, which in turn, impose stress and career barriers. Finally, given the turmoil created by these issues, this book will also provide context for psychologists, social workers, counsellors, and psychotherapists who provide mental health support to the people who are dealing with these all-consuming career-related barriers and setbacks.

In many ways, I also help people steer through many work-related problems, and business and leadership obstacles. I help direct the take-off of careers, and more importantly, to make those transitions as smooth as possible, and ensure that clients land safely in the right work roles without the dreaded crash landings.

In this book, I am consolidating essential career advice that draws on the wisdom of I/O Psychology and what I've learned through working in the field for 20+ years to navigate crucial work scenarios and make high-stakes employment and leadership decisions. My intention is to support you by sharing what I've learned and my best advice. Since many of my clients come to me when they've already tried other options to resolve their complicated problems, I have been playing in the big leagues and have seen and done a lot that will never show up in a Google search. In essence, what I share in this book will equip you with a knowledge base to make informed decisions around building and sustaining a resilient career.

After coaching countless clients, writing blog articles, developing training materials, offering workshops, and delivering talks, I've assembled the most important takeaways into a digestible and relatable package. I begin the book by explaining how I start to work with clients by administering psychometric assessments. These are standardized methods used to measure individuals' mental capabilities and behavioral style. Psychometric testing measures candidates' suitability for a role based on the required personality characteristics and aptitude (or cognitive abilities).

My preferred assessments are beyond the financial means of some of my clients but when these assessments are feasible, I believe that they are invaluable. The reasons behind my enthusiasm about these tools are simple. All of us have biases and sometimes our biases lead us to inaccurate assumptions about ourselves and our circumstances. In this book, after I explain the basics of psychometric assessments, I describe each of the ten most commonly faced issues that my clients deal with. They are disruptive career experiences, and they have multiple interconnected layers, making them complex and difficult to navigate. A lack of awareness around these career derailers can threaten a person's livelihood, profoundly impacting their financial security and identity. This is why I have taken care to offer insights and nuanced perspectives that are rooted in my experience, but also incorporate research and experts I've consulted in other fields including employment law, human rights law, union leadership, etc.

Incidents or crises that threaten to disrupt someone's career are often kept in the dark. These scenarios are not always discussed even though they can be catastrophic. Sometimes the act of signing a non-disclosure agreement (NDA) keeps people from telling their story. Other times, silence is kept because the person who has experienced a significant hardship or setback does not want to burn any bridges by explaining what really happened. There are also times where someone feels embarrassment or shame because of what they have experienced. In my mind, this is the worst (yet understandable) reason for keeping quiet. The troublemaker or aggressor should be the one who feels shame, not the victim.

For the next several chapters, I will address these common internally disruptive career experiences. Usually, I focus on the employee's perspective but sometimes, when it's helpful, I will also include the HR or organizational perspective. When I share the organizational, HR, or business owner's perspective, it is so that you can understand the "other side" and govern yourself accordingly.

I am grateful that I have worked with a full spectrum of clients over the years. Although I have always been based in Canada, I have supported clients who were based in the United States, the United Arab Emirates, South Africa, Ghana, Saudi Arabia, Germany, and elsewhere. As a result of where and how I grew up, I understand the typical or dominant white culture and perspective that is most prevalent in North America. Through the experiences of colleagues, friends, and family who live in Europe and Australia, I understand that although the accents differ, the experiences of people who are in racial, religious, or other underrepresented groups are similar, regardless of the country. As a Black, Canadian-born woman with parents who were born in Jamaica and Ghana, West Africa, I also understand what it is like to navigate the professional work world as a "racialized" person. I use quotations because although every race is a race – including Caucasians – as a result of how Black, Indigenous, and people of color have been designated as "other races" or we've been "racialized" relative to the white majorities in North America and Western Europe, I have an intimate understanding of how this plays out in many workplaces. Although most of this book is independent of the reader's ethnicity, where possible, I also offer insights that should resonate with racialized or Black, Indigenous, or people of color (BIPOC) readers. Or to use the terminology that's more familiar to European readers BAME – which is an acronym for Black, Asian, minority ethnic or even BME, a shorter variant for Black and minority ethnic. To make these insights easier to find, they may be treated as a sidebar of sorts. The sidebar treatment does not imply that these commentaries are less important, but rather addresses the fact that some people need different or additional information that can be extremely hard to find.

Whether you are already in a career or you are deciding on a career, the information that I will share in this book will help you. Naturally, as a book, the information is unidirectional. The information flows from me to you. I offer a wealth of information that will be useful when you are bouncing back after a setback or trying to prevent setbacks. In many ways, this is the book that I wish existed when I was starting my career or when I experienced challenges in my career. Despite my ties to the academic world, I have always applied what I know about psychology in a practical and relatable way. That tradition will continue in this book.

Although there's value in reading *How to Be Resilient in Your Career: Facing Up to Barriers at Work* from cover to cover, given how full most professional people's lives are, I have tried to structure this book so that you can read the chapters in isolation (or out of order) and focus on the parts that match your circumstances the best.

CHAPTER 1

Psychometric Testing

I am including this chapter so that readers who need to complete psychometric tests as part of a hiring or career development process will have a clearer understanding of what they are and how the results may be used.

As a Work and Business Psychologist, I have seen the immense value of using psychometric testing to support my clients' efforts. Psychometric tests provide test-takers with objective feedback about themselves. Depending on the test, it can give insights into someone's personality and how that may impact their relationships with their peers, subordinates, superiors, clients, etc. In terms of personality tests, I prefer those that measure or are linked to the "Big Five" Factors or traits of personality sometimes known by the acronym OCEAN or CANOE. Regardless of the preferred acronym, the letters stand for Openness to experience (intellectually curious, imaginative, and spontaneous vs. practical, conventional, and preferring routine), Conscientiousness (disciplined, dependable, and careful vs. spontaneous and disorganized), Extraversion (warm, sociable, and emotionally expressive vs. reserved and thoughtful), Agreeableness (trusting, helpful, and empathetic vs. critical, suspicious, and uncooperative), and Neuroticism (anxious and prone to negative emotions vs. calm, even-tempered, and secure). Each of us will fall somewhere on a continuum for each of these traits and these qualities are stable across our lifetime.

When I'm working with professionals (i.e., people who are sought out because of their subject matter expertise or "thought leadership"), business owners, aspiring executives, or executives, I usually start with an assessment that captures the OCEAN dimensions in the context of their role

DOI: 10.4324/9781003328988-2

and what's being demanded of them at work. This is also an excellent starting point when a client is contemplating a career change, but they are not sure which direction would suit them best.

Whether I'm working with a dyad, a team, the C-Suite, or a board of directors, it is ideal to build in representation from each major "type" of person and have all the key areas covered. The rationale is that each group can only have a "whole brain" if each of the parts of the brain is represented by the members. If one perspective, approach, or style of thinking is missing, the group will be incomplete and vulnerable to making mistakes. It's hard to overstate the value of this approach when an organization needs to avoid blind spots and try to see around corners. Furthermore, greater self-awareness is always helpful when we are interacting with others so that we have a better appreciation for how our behaviors may impact the people with whom we're interacting.

The advantage of psychometric assessments is that these tests provide an objective foundation that should be relatively free of a client's biases and/or "head trash." I also like them since, for so many people, their colleagues, clients, and superiors are too busy and generally unwilling to provide concrete feedback that is specific enough to be useful.

Although in my practice I often start with a psychometric assessment, in a book, that is impractical. I am intentionally refraining from recommending specific assessments because there are many options out there – some good, others that are harder to recommend. Also, testing is an extremely lucrative industry. This means that many of these assessments are expensive and linked to powerful interests and their lawyers. Obviously, I need to tread carefully.

What I can suggest is checking in with your career center for alumni (or students) from the college or university that you attended (are attending). Often, they'll be able to provide you with free or cost-effective assessments that you can use as your starting point. If those advisors are well trained on the assessment tools, they can help you interpret your results.

Once you are armed with better self-awareness, you're positioned for better performance.

As implied previously, psychometric testing is a huge industry. Some tests are free, and others must be paid for and used under specific circumstances. The latter, more expensive assessments are administered and interpreted by people with an MA or PhD in Psychology (or similar background). Naturally, some of the free/cheaper tests are popular (e.g., Sixteen Personality Factor Questionnaire (16PF), DISC, and Myers-Briggs "lite" variants, etc.) while others seem obscure to the general population.

Many of these tests have been criticized as being part of pseudo-science where invalidated opinions have been falsely equated with facts. When this happens "for fun" by or with individuals, it can be harmless. But, when tests with questionable reliability (i.e., consistency) and validity (i.e., it measures what it's supposed to measure) are used to make decisions about who should be hired or promoted, it's a much more serious problem.

Sometimes, psychometric testing is used to make hiring decisions. This can be risky since not all tests are reliable or valid – especially when used in ways that were not anticipated by the test developers. In a world full of companies that are determined to use "big data" to identify potential candidates in a cost-effective manner, things can go sideways. If you're required to complete this type of testing, then I suggest that you try to answer honestly, since trying to "game" the test may trigger high scores on hidden validity sub-scales embedded in the test. If it's clear that you've been "faking good" or that you've been very defensive (i.e., trying to downplay or hide something), then your results may not be interpretable. Worse yet, the potential employer might assume that you've got something to hide and screen you out.

I caution my Human Resources (HR) clients to only use psychometric testing as part of their evaluation or hiring process, not their main/only evaluation. Understandably, some candidates get very nervous during high-stakes evaluations. If they never get a chance to speak for themselves or show what they're capable of then it could result in lost opportunities – for employers and candidates.

I am a big advocate for using psychometric testing for nonthreatening professional development. I prefer that results are shared with test-takers using their personal email addresses so that the results remain private unless the test-taker chooses to share their private results. This allows test-takers to get better insights about themselves and they can make use of opportunities to become better individual contributors, leaders, or executives. That creates true win/win situations for employers and employees.

Psychometric testing is a huge topic with broad implications. In my experience, it's often a relevant and appropriate starting point in the context of a career change, leadership development, working as an executive or an executive coach, becoming an entrepreneur, or evaluating a potential franchisee. In each of these situations, the person taking (or using) the test can gain valuable insights that are hard to come by otherwise. These insights will help the test-taker work in ways that suit their strengths and develop strategies to work around their weaknesses or blind spots.

LEADERSHIP ASSESSMENTS

I use leadership assessments, a sub-category of psychometric assessments, with many of my professional and executive clients. The paid assessments that I use are suitable for professionals who are leaders in their fields (i.e., "thought leaders") who others seek out for their subject matter expertise. The assessments that I use are also suitable for "traditional" leaders who have other people reporting directly to them (i.e., "direct reports").

I believe that all leaders can gain valuable perspectives about their strengths and their "blind spots" by completing a leadership assessment and getting some related coaching. Our strengths are sometimes more self-evident than our weaknesses. I often use the term blind spots or vulnerabilities instead of weaknesses because these are problematic behaviors that arise during times of stress, fatigue, boredom, strain, etc. These may even be behaviors that are strengths when things are going well. Once armed with the leadership assessment results, it is much easier to find and implement strategies to work around these blind spots or vulnerabilities through planning and learning (e.g., reading, podcasts, videos, practice, on-the-job tasks/assignments, etc.). This can be especially useful for new leaders or executives who are facing an especially challenging assignment or mandate.

It can take one to three years for an emerging or developing manager to become fully effective. When you invest in Leadership and Executive Coaching, you should work together with your coach to create a road map or to navigate events and challenges that use your strengths and avoid activating the vulnerabilities identified during the assessment. You will take the right steps, and you and your coach should track milestones to measure your progress.

Normally, when working with my clients, I offer feedback based on their assessment results but of course, that step is not possible in a book.

Regardless of whether you want to take any psychometric assessments or not, almost every professional will benefit from understanding how to address serious, commonly faced workplace challenges. The ten problems that I will cover in this book are significant career derailers that are serious enough that they can hurt your career progression and, therefore, limit your income. Despite their prevalence, most of these problems aren't openly discussed nor is it easy to see how they resolve since often non-disclosure agreements (NDAs) are signed by the people hurt in these situations keeping their testimony hidden.

Now that we've covered the essentials related to psychometric assessments, let's move into the main reasons why people seek me out – serious, but frequently experienced career dilemmas that many talented professionals face.

CHAPTER 2

Underemployment or Being Overqualified

The vast majority of my coaching clients are well educated and talented, yet sometimes, they have been underemployed. As a result of my experiences with them, I have developed a deep understanding of how some people become and/or remain underemployed. Without assigning blame to the underemployed or overqualified, in this chapter, I will explain some of the hidden consequences and offer suggestions for finding roles that are better aligned with one's abilities.

One of the most common problems that I help clients with is underemployment or being overqualified. Underemployment is when you're working less than you'd like to or earning less than you should, given your level of experience, skills, or credentials and education. Examples include someone who chronically only works part-time hours despite wanting to work full-time hours and someone who has a university degree in engineering but works at a photocopy center or coffee shop for minimum wage. If my examples seem oddly specific, it's because I've made small talk with university-educated engineers who were helping me with orders at my local copy center and coffee shops in recent years.

Being overqualified is when you are just too good for the job – you have way more experience and/or more education than is needed or appropriate for the role. For instance, there is an opening for a paramedic in your city but someone who is qualified to be the head physician for the Department of Emergency Medicine is willing to take the job because they need to work while waiting for their accreditation to work as a physician from another jurisdiction to be approved in their new jurisdiction.

DOI: 10.4324/9781003328988-3

Many people hire me because they are underemployed despite their education or work experience. Sometimes they are newcomers who earned their professional credentials in another country. Often, however, people contact me because they intentionally acquired additional qualifications so that they could get a foot in the door in the workforce. They were led to believe that they were not getting job offers because they lacked something that the more successful candidates had. Still, other times someone started to work at a company or organization years ago and despite learning and improving on the job, they have remained stuck in a lower-level role. They have worked hard to get a solid education and have been performing effectively for years without the rewards that should have come their way by now – sometimes 8–10 years or more without a formal promotion or a meaningful pay bump. There is a lot to unpack.

OVERQUALIFIED AND UNDEREMPLOYED: BIG EGO OR REAL PROBLEM?

Many of us grew up being told that we were wonderful and can do anything that we set our minds to. Sometimes this is true, and we have unlimited potential and abilities. This may leave us feeling overqualified for our jobs. If we feel overqualified, does it mean that we actually are?

In 2014, *Time* magazine[1] reported that 36% of survey respondents in a study of over 700 employees believed they were overqualified for their current jobs, and about two-thirds of those were searching for a new role that would be a better fit for their skills. This pattern has persisted – and seems to be worsening. According to I-Heng (Ray) Wu, a doctoral student in the Department of Management and Entrepreneurship[2] at the Tippie College of Business, an employee's perception of their own overqualification is a significant problem for businesses. In his dissertation research, he cites a 2017 Gallup Poll that demonstrated that 68% of U.S. college graduates across a range of professions think they have more education than is needed for their job.

Consider these criteria to help you decide whether you're overqualified or underemployed.

You're bored. Boredom is a common sign that you're overqualified. Sometimes this happens when you're not being challenged or stretched. You feel like you've been there and done that. If you can manage your work half asleep or with one proverbial hand tied behind your back, you're probably overqualified. But boredom could also be a signal that you're in the wrong job because the job might be a bad fit. It's important to figure out whether it's a bad fit or if you're overqualified. Either way, it might be wise to start considering alternative employment or a different role in the same organization, if that's an option.

You legitimately know as much or more than your boss. If you're getting more and/or better results than what's expected for someone in your role to the extent that people turn to you instead of your manager/boss for direction and advice, then you're probably overqualified.

You're often looking for more work to do. You typically finish your work quickly and then find something else that needs to be done and do it even though it's not in your job description. Sometimes you'll ask your boss what else you can do. If you keep getting the message that your employer doesn't need or want you to do more and has no ideas for what you can do, it means you've already gone above and beyond what the job requires. In other words, you're overqualified.

You're not developing or learning. Ideally, when you start a new job, there's a steep learning curve. You need to learn new things in order to be successful. You're exhausted at the end of most days and/or at the end of the week. If, however, you're able to perform a new job well without any training or guidance, you're probably overqualified for it. You probably won't have much room to grow in that role. Also, if you have way more experience than the job description requires, you could be overqualified. It's possible to have more education than is required for the role but *not* be overqualified.

Education isn't always the same or better than relevant work experience.

Your salary has plateaued. You've been working hard in the same role, taking on challenging projects, and getting favorable feedback about the quality of your work. If despite these positives, you haven't received a meaningful salary increase in a few years, you might be underemployed. In some fields, 2% to 3% annual raises are common, in other fields, it could be as much as 5% to 10%. Over time, these add up. Do some research to determine the current market value for your level of skills and experience in your region. If you're earning below what the market pays, it may be worth re-evaluating.

IMPLICATIONS OF BEING OVERQUALIFIED

When you're pigeon-holed, it becomes difficult to be seen in a different light. So, when you're an engineer who works in a retail job at the local photocopy center, if you stay in that role long enough, you're seen as a photocopier, not as an engineer. Others who see you in this role that's below your abilities may eventually assume that your role is consistent with your abilities. What's potentially worse is that you may start to see that your "lower than it should be role" is your "real" level. You may lower your own internal standards and expectations.

If possible, you should plan to leave a job for which you are overqualified so that you can avoid being sidelined into an unsuitable role for the long term. Being overqualified often means that you're underemployed … working, but not earning what you should be earning. This isn't trivial. Compounded over the long term, underemployment can have a negative impact on your lifelong earnings and standard of living. When the gap between your actual earnings and your potential earnings is wide, and your low pay makes it difficult to pay off student loans and/or other debts while sustaining other aspects of your life, the financial stress can take a toll on your mental and physical health.

There is also a link between current and future salary that isn't helpful when you're underemployed. Often, during negotiations, your current salary is used as a baseline to anchor what your new employer will offer to pay you. When you have an unreasonably low baseline or current salary, it's harder to negotiate a more appropriate salary.

When you do not use your skills, they may become stale or outdated, especially in fields that are constantly evolving (e.g., engineering, computer science, etc.). Moreover, for certain jobs, the hiring manager or employer may require that your experience is recent (i.e., within the past 2–3 years). So, your hard-earned, but underused work experience may not count as "recent enough" to get you screened in for future opportunities.

THE ONE THAT GOT AWAY: BEING PASSED OVER FOR PROMOTION

Sometimes you can be hired into an organization at an appropriate level but then your career can stall, and you can remain stuck at one level. When this happens, being overqualified or underemployed is something that kind of creeps up on you. This can happen when you are passed over again and again for roles that you can perform well if you were given the chance. Sadly, when you are passed over often enough, you become underemployed and overqualified. This is an extremely common scenario for many women and BIPOC/ BAME employees – so common that I could almost say that it's universal. Despite the prevalence of this problem, very few people want to write about it or offer solutions.

Starting in the summer of 2020 following the murder of George Floyd and the social justice protests that started all over the world, great attention has been paid to systemic racism, a reminder that people of color are less represented as one climbs up the corporate ladder. This means that most Black, Indigenous, and people of color (BIPOC) have experienced being passed over for a promotion they believed was deserved.

Members of the BIPOC/BAME communities are familiar with the expression "we've got to work twice as hard to get half as far" as our white counterparts. This sentiment has been expressed repeatedly by Michelle Obama[3] and most other parents within these communities. Since childhood, we've known that we'll never get in the door without solid qualifications.

A common narrative or subtext is that racialized job candidates and employees are unqualified, and they only get opportunities because quotas need to be filled. In other words, they are tokens rather than qualified. Contrary to popular opinion, and based on what I've seen up close, in many fields including accounting, nursing, medicine, engineering, and computer science, racialized people are overrepresented relative to their numbers in the general population. This survey of visible minority university students[4] shows that they make up a significant percentage of the campus population. In 2019, The Association of American Colleges and Universities reported that racialized students made up 45.2% of the undergraduate student population in 2016. BIPOC students made up 32.0% of the graduate student population in 2016.

The state of most workplaces suggests that something other than merit is operating – or we would see better representation at all levels.

The U.S. college admissions scandal that came to light in 2019 – whereby celebrities and other wealthy people took action to get preferential treatment for their children – is a great example of how widespread and well established the practice of passing over has become. It's hard to know how many better-qualified candidates were passed over and denied opportunities because some parents used their money to pave the way for their kids' success.

Here are two examples of how being passed over plays out in the workplace. One scenario that I've heard from BAME/ BIPOC men and women is that they've been asked to train someone who eventually becomes his/her boss, or who took their job *before* they were planning to leave. The other variant is when someone less experienced and less capable gets a promotion over a colleague who was qualified in every way. Regardless of which version someone experiences of being passed over, it's incredibly discouraging and painful.

Other surprisingly common reasons for being passed over for promotion in even the most professional-seeming organizations include favoritism and nepotism. In certain organizations, promotions are based on intentional or unintentional favoritism. It can be a convenient method for deciding who to promote and assign other rewards like preferred files, clients, etc. but it contributes to a negative corporate culture. This issue is described as cronyism and nepotism and it's classified as a key aspect of a non-inclusive workplace. The lack of inclusion is one of the main drivers identified in research by Sull, Sull, Cipolli, and Brighenti (2022),[5] fueling the great resignation. I'll return to and expand on workplace inclusion in Chapter 7 "Identity Is Complex."

ADVICE FOR WHEN YOU'VE BEEN PASSED OVER

While an emotional response is natural for being passed over, it is important to take a day or two to process and calm down, and not exhibit an openly emotional response to the situation. To lose your temper or have an emotional meltdown in front of your employer will only reaffirm that he/she made the right choice.

Understand that being passed over for a promotion is not always a sign of failure. There can be a myriad of reasons someone else made the cut. The reasons may not be what you think. When you are ready to receive feedback, you should ask for a feedback session or informal conversation about why you were overlooked for promotion.

I had a client who was passed over for a position she really wanted. She had been sure she was in line for a job doing member outreach for a union.

I had done everything right. Then a much younger woman was chosen for the position. She was at least ten years younger than me. I asked the decision-maker to tell me the truth. Was I passed over because I was older, more outspoken, maybe seen as a troublemaker with too many opinions? The look of surprise on the manager's face told me immediately I was wrong. "Not at all," she told me. "We chose Chloe for member outreach because she speaks five languages."

Chloe's manager offered a direct response to her question. However, one bona fide red flag is vague feedback. If your boss can't give you valid reasons why you didn't make the cut, there could be factors at work that are beyond your control. Make sure you keep a record of any formal communication and note anything your employer or supervisor says to you. In that conversation, ask how you can improve or work differently. If your supervisor can't offer constructive, useful advice, maybe it's time to start looking for your next job with some help from a career coach who can help you determine your next best move.

I fully acknowledge that there are countless times when extraordinarily capable people are passed over for promotions – and truly mediocre people get those coveted opportunities. My comments are not meant to deny those situations or gaslight anyone. Once you've taken some time to cool down and process what has happened, you'll be in a better position to determine whether you were passed over for legitimate and justifiable reasons or whether you were passed over because of some aspect of your identity that should be irrelevant in the context of your workplace performance.

NO NEED TO HELP AN EMPLOYER SCREEN YOU OUT

There are times when your underemployment or being overqualified persists because you don't apply for all the opportunities that you could. I don't say this to lay the blame on you. Rather, I'm reflecting on another problem that I see often whereby someone wants to apply for a job that they know they can do but their expertise and/or credentials are different from what is listed in the job posting. A recent experience was a vivid reminder of how, when applying for certain jobs, we should apply even when our credentials are different than what is "required." Sometimes employers are not aware of alternative ways that candidates can be qualified to fill a particular role. When presented with unexpected, but appropriate qualifications, education, and skills, a well-written cover letter or a simple conversation can prevent a strong candidate from being screened out.

SOMETIMES, DIFFERENT IS BETTER

Over the years, several people have asked me why I don't have a coaching certificate offered by the International Coach Federation (ICF), the Professional Certified Coach (PCC) certificate, or one of the others. I always enjoy answering those questions. On the one hand, it's smart that organizations and consumers are starting to insist on certain credentials. The business, life, and career coaching industries are unregulated so it's helpful that some minimum standards are being imposed. The problem is that these minimum standards don't always match up with the needs of people who are searching for services. There are times when people can qualify for a certificate yet still not offer an effective service to their clients. Moreover, there are times when a different foundation is an even better match for a client's needs.

So, here's why my qualifications are different from most career coaches (and HR consultants). Several years ago, I made the strategic decision to continue to base my professional services on my PhD in Industrial and Organizational (I/O) Psychology, commonly known as Work or Business Psychology. I know that it's a clunky title, but when you scratch the surface and consider the implications of my degrees and 20 years of relevant professional experience, there's plenty of depth and versatility there that suits my clients' needs and interests.

I was approached by a company based in another country that provides specialized telehealth services to clients via computers and/or mobile devices. They were expanding into Canada and wanted to have a local career coach to provide services to their clients. In principle, I was interested.

This company was searching for career coaches who were qualified, so they wanted to find someone who was *"certified,"* since that was their proxy for competence. That made good sense. They started the conversation by insisting on a popular coaching designation. I explained my alternative designations and the rationale for them. I clarified that, although my qualifications (a PhD in Psychology and registration in a professional college) don't match their expectations, my credentials and expertise are actually *harder to acquire.* More importantly, I achieve desirable results when working with my clients. I also explained what it means to be a member of a professional college and the implications in terms of liability and accountability (plus coverage by insurance under certain circumstances).

I share this recent experience for two reasons: First, sometimes when you apply for a position your credentials may be different from what's expected but that doesn't mean that the story must end there. There are many well-intentioned people who write job postings that are more like a wish list than a list of what's necessary. In some of these situations, there may not be anyone who meets all the criteria. In addition, sometimes, different is better.

If your unique background is truly a good fit for an employer's needs, you should make your case. For example, imagine that a university was looking for a professor to teach creative writing to a first-year English class. All the typical applicants with PhDs may have studied all the great works and many will have published academic articles. In practice, however, are they the best choices to instruct on how to be an effective *creative* writer?

What about a successful novelist with over ten books published who has offered writing workshops – but has not earned a PhD? If I was a creative writing student, I might prefer to learn from someone who has done what I aspire to do.

To me, the screening out of a potential candidate because their qualifications do not match up with the anticipated requirements can be problematic and short-sighted. In this example, students would probably learn more from a successful writer who has applied their talent rather than one who is well read on the subject but has no relevant applied or lived experience. If that published writer said to me, "I'm not sure I should apply for that instructor position," I would definitely encourage them to apply.

Second, if you don't make your case, you'll never know what could have been possible – and there's not much to lose by explaining how your alternative qualifications meet an employer's needs. If the novelist doesn't approach the university to express their interest, it's a missed opportunity for the novelist, the students, and the university.

Many business owners, hiring managers, and HR personnel are in the habit of looking for the same types of candidates that they have always hired. In many situations, that's a reasonable starting point, but it's also very limited. I'll also say that when strong candidates who are "uniquely qualified" never present themselves, to some extent, they share some blame for restricting their own opportunities.

I'm not one of those people who says one thing but does another. I walk the talk. I've had similar experiences with organizations that were looking for executive coaches for their leaders. Sometimes, they will insist on some type of certification. If I have the time, I'll explain my credentials, experience, and registration with a professional college and how all of that far exceeds what they say they are looking for. More often than not, when a human is able to participate in a phone call or an email exchange instead of software impersonating a human, they usually find a workaround so that I can be their resource.

Note – While I stand behind the arguments made in this chapter, I fully understand that there are some situations where being "uniquely qualified" isn't adequate because of laws and/or regulations that govern specific professions (e.g., many health-related occupations, law, engineering, teaching, etc.).

Over the years, I have noticed that many professionals are careful about who they seek advice and support from. This makes sense since most of us are careful about who we will hire to fix our cars, provide our medical care, or give us legal advice. Career coaching for professionals is qualitatively different from career coaching for people who didn't need to earn professional or post-graduate training in order to enter their field.

If I were a lawyer contemplating some professional changes to my career, there is no way that I'd hire someone "off the Internet" whose own educational and professional history is unclear or considerably weaker and less lucrative than mine was. I'd also want to find and hire someone who was successful in their profession before they started offering their coaching services.

DOES A DEGREE STILL GUARANTEE EMPLOYMENT?

I have worked with countless clients who have earned advanced degrees. In the past, having a professional degree in engineering, law, or teaching, etc. or a graduate degree practically guaranteed stable and lucrative employment. There was no question that the investment of your time and money in school would pay off. Somehow, for some professionals and aspiring professionals, those days of guaranteed, high-quality employment seem elusive.

If you're a professional/aspiring professional who has earned the right credentials, but you can't get a stronghold in the job market – you may be asking yourself "now what?" Or you may be a parent who has invested time and money raising and educating your kids and you're extremely disappointed to see them underemployed for no fault of their own.

ACADEMIC INFLATION

I'll admit that if I was in school right now, I'm not sure that I'd spend the time required to earn my doctorate in psychology. Don't get me wrong, I do value the foundation that I built by studying psychology at a high level. I appreciate the fact that I grew accustomed to figuring things out when there is no clear answer (this is part of the territory when you earn a PhD). Despite those benefits, it's apparent that things have changed since I was a student. It's more expensive and there's lots of talk about "academic inflation" – whereby degrees seem less valuable because they are plentiful. Regardless of these real and imagined changes in the economy, paid employment is still necessary for most of us.

Given these challenges, it's no surprise that most of my career-coaching clients are professionals or aspiring professionals. Sometimes clients reach out to me themselves, other times, especially clients who are still in their twenties, their parents contact me first. They tell me that one of the things they find encouraging is that they are confident that I have enough experience to be able to help solve major challenges. Further, in an unregulated field where anyone can build a website and call themselves a career coach or a life coach, it's hard to tell the difference between coaches who are great at marketing versus those who can deliver results.

In many cases, the best option is to find ways to reframe a client's skills and experience so that they resonate more with potential employers. That, combined with strategic ways to gain access to employment opportunities, is often all that's required.

There are, however, other situations where the most viable long-term option is self-employment or entrepreneurship. When a capable recent grad is faced with the prospects of precarious contract work or numerous unpaid internships, the prospect of building their own business or buying a franchise becomes very compelling. Similarly, for a more mature and experienced person who needs to find a different path forward, building a business or buying a franchise becomes much more attractive. This is even more so when they are already at the top end of the pay scale and future employers are closer to their children's age than the age of their peers.

Common myths around business/franchise ownership often mean that it's an overlooked option. Self-employment, entrepreneurship, and franchise ownership isn't for everyone, but it can be appealing when there's a good alignment of interests, skills, and personal qualities … plus favorable financial circumstances.

UNDEREMPLOYMENT CAN BE A GOOD THING … SOMETIMES

Typically, we are encouraged to: Get ahead! Get promoted! Make more money! Aim higher! Unsurprisingly, clients often come to me to find out how to move ahead. It is rare that I counsel a client to aim for less.

With that said, there are times when I come across a situation in which working below full capacity is an appropriate response – when there's a good reason behind it. New parents come to mind, as do newcomers who are adjusting to a new culture and a new way of life. For example, when a parent of young children has just moved to a new country and they are preoccupied with learning where everything is in their new city, helping their children adapt to new routines, new people, and coping with the loss of their previous way of life, while working and doing their own adjusting and mourning – it is all a daunting challenge. In a perfect world, they would only need to work part-time (or less) during this transition. Or, if this parent was working full-time, I can see how working below their full capacity could be appealing for the short term.

So, although chronic underemployment is often terrible on multiple levels, in the short term, I've seen it work to an employee's advantage. As we saw during the Covid-19 pandemic, trying to parent, support online learning, and work, while surviving, it was tempting (and often appropriate) to find a way to cut back on work responsibilities. Another scenario that comes to mind is the challenge of being part of the sandwich generation and needing more time and energy to devote to helping senior parents.

I believe that under certain circumstances, being overqualified can sometimes work to your advantage in the short term – when work–life balance is impossible – but tread carefully, because there can be a long-term impact.

When you are taking a step back or accepting roles that are too junior for you, your future employer may worry that hiring you is a mistake because you will not stick around. To overcome objections that you're overqualified and may not stay, highlight your attributes and how they will benefit the organization. Your experience and skill set mean less training time and increased productivity. Also, consider repositioning or reframing your overqualification by noting that you are fully qualified for the tasks that are most important in the role.

As noted earlier in this chapter, I don't recommend long-term underemployment because of the link between current and future salary. Another reason why underemployment is problematic is because when you find yourself in a role that's below your abilities – and you have been in that role for too long – you may lower your own internal standards and expectations for yourself.

In addition, underemployment is not ideal because when you don't use your skills and keep up with your field, you can fall behind. Your skills become stale and underused. Then, when you decide you're ready to go back into your field or seek a promotion, you may find your work experience and skills are not recent enough to get you screened-in for certain opportunities.

If you decide to go this way, and take a job where you'll be underemployed, try to create a plan – and set a reminder – so that this doesn't go on for much longer than it should because of the consequences on your career mobility and income. If you're not sure you have the bandwidth or you want to create some built-in accountability, consider talking to an experienced career coach or advisor to help you devise a strategy. Ideally, you can plan so that underemployment remains reversible, or a stepping stone that leads you to something favorable on an appropriate timeline.

If possible, you should plan to leave a job for which you are overqualified so that you can avoid being sidelined into an unsuitable role for the long term.

But, if we feel overqualified, does it mean that we are? Depending on who you are, yes, you probably are over-qualified. Some estimate that over 40% of university gradu-ates are overqualified, and it can be even worse for people with a graduate degree. Similarly, Black, Indigenous, and people of color (BIPOC) employees/BAME (Black, Asian, minority ethnic) employees are often overrepresented on the lower rungs of the corporate ladder and deal with the conse-quences of underemployment. Often, just to get onto the first rung of the corporate ladder, they have more experience or more credentials than their non-racialized peers, so in some ways, they are set up for underemployment from day one in some roles.

THE UNDEREMPLOYMENT TRAP FOR THE IMMIGRANT OR NEWCOMER

Sometimes, the underemployed people who I work with are newcomers or immigrants. For the sake of this section, I may use the term "newcomer" and "immigrant" interchangeably. If this doesn't describe you then you'll want to skim or even skip this section.

It takes incredible courage to leave one's home country and move to a new country. It can take several years of planning and preparation since immigration applications can require years to be reviewed and processed before being approved. Then, once you arrive in your new country, a whole new set of challenges begins.

Newcomers I have worked with are often racialized and/ or have accents that stand out. Invariably, these racialized newcomers often know that to get a foot in the door to get "local" experience, they need to be twice as good as their white counterparts. Unfortunately, they often come to the realization that, after they get their foot in the door, they remain underemployed and under-earning.

We've all heard the anecdotes. Doctors driving taxis or working for Uber, engineers working in call centers. Newcomers often find it incredibly difficult to find employment that is commensurate with the skills and credentials obtained in another country.

Consequently, many newcomers decide to focus on self-employment, instead of trying to get back into their previous professions, since their foreign-earned credentials aren't always accepted. In some ways, self-employment can be less risky than finding a traditional job if your skills and abilities are undervalued.

To be fair, however, self-employment and entrepreneurship can be extremely difficult, especially in the first few years. Native-born early-stage entrepreneurs often need support to develop sustainable business plans and business models. Then there's the challenge of growing a professional network. All of these issues can be compounded for newcomers who are still adjusting to life in a new country with few social or professional connections.

It's difficult to determine why some newcomers become very successful in their new country while others don't fare very well. A visit to any Dunkin' Donuts, Tim Horton's, or other franchise coffee shop/fast food venue or Walmart/ large-scale store will show you where many immigrants start their careers, despite having earned diplomas or degrees from post-secondary institutions. Stories of foreign-trained physicians, lawyers, and other professionals who successfully navigated the steps necessary to obtain a license to practice in their chosen fields in their new countries are much rarer.

The valuable education and training that newcomers have acquired have made them eligible to immigrate. When you're a professional newcomer (e.g., physician, nurse, academic, lawyer, engineer, etc.), it's essential that you are strategic while re-establishing yourself in a new country. Here are some best practices to help you get started.

ADVICE FOR THE NEWCOMER TO CONSIDER BEFORE ARRIVAL

- Update your résumé or collect all the information that you'll need to write one when the time is right. For example, put together the names of the organizations where you've worked, the years that you worked there, what you accomplished in those roles, proof of the degrees and/or other certifications that you've earned.
- If feasible, create or update your LinkedIn profile. It doesn't need to be perfect, even a strong profile is a work-in-progress that will evolve as your career evolves.
- While you're updating your LinkedIn profile, try to get former bosses, clients, and colleagues to write recommendations on your behalf. This will be helpful if future employers don't want to contact your references who may be based in different time zones or may be difficult to reach because of the costs associated with overseas phone calls.
- It's essential that you set yourself up to be able to do video and/or audio interviews via Zoom, Google Meet, Skype, or FaceTime. The global pandemic has made video interviews very common – even for local employees. This is a real silver lining for candidates who are not local but are willing to relocate if necessary. This may mean planning for higher-speed Internet and backup power sources to offset intermittent or rolling blackouts.
- Start reading career and human resources (HR) websites and blogs so that you can get a sense of how things operate in the country that you'll be moving to, and how that new workplace is similar to or different from the workplace in your country of origin.
- By all means, use the internet to find other relevant resources, but also consider reading my *Career Development,*

Career Management, and HR blog[6] for the North American context. It's searchable by voice or by typing keywords and there are over 200 articles.

- In addition, you may wish to read past issues of my bi-monthly newsletter[7] (and if you like what you see, go to the URL in this endnote to subscribe[8]).

ADVICE FOR THE NEWCOMER TO CONSIDER AFTER ARRIVAL

- Do what's necessary to get yourself and your family settled. You may be preoccupied and less at ease until this happens. Further, without those basics in place, many other things will be even more difficult.
- Find ways to get yourself integrated within the broader community; and there are countless resources about this on the internet, including on my blog.
- To the extent that it's possible, avoid accepting work roles that are too far below your capacity since you may face negative consequences if you are wrongly categorized or stereotyped. Many well-intentioned organizations provide free advice about getting established in the workforce. Don't fall prey to the assumption that the only roles that newcomers can acquire to get local experience are in minimum wage service jobs at fast food or retail establishments.
- Consider strategic volunteering and/or self-employment as tactical ways to gain local experience.

AVOID THE NEWCOMER CRASH

Ever since I started working with newcomers, I have been reflecting on why some are super successful while others never reclaim their status and potential after moving to a new country.

One time I was taking an Uber somewhere because I didn't want to drive due to inconvenient parking. The drive started off with the usual pleasantries, "Nice weather we are having, much better than yesterday ..." – but for whatever reason, this man decided to ask me what I do for a living. When I told him I was an HR consultant and career coach, he immediately replied with a chuckle, "I wish I'd have known you and consulted with you last year! Now I'm stuck driving this car 15 hours a day just to support my family."

Suddenly, the intensity of our conversation picked up. He began to describe his biggest professional mistake which deeply affected his personal life. He had hastily left his stable job as a city bus driver to pursue what he thought would be a great career opportunity in another country.

To paraphrase him:

> I was miserable driving that bus. Ten years of doing the same route, working split shifts which meant very long hours, not getting to see my kids as often as I'd like, and my poor wife was never able to book a vacation for us during the holidays. I needed a change. I'm from Lebanon and had not been back to see my family in years. My parents have never met their grandchildren, so when I met a businessman who offered to start a bakery in Dubai that I would operate, I jumped at the opportunity. It would mean being closer to my relatives and closer to my culture. Plus, of course, I'd be doing something that I actually love. My true passion is owning a small business and making food.

Unfortunately, this is not where my Uber driver's story ended. So far, there is no happily ever after ending for this hard-working person. No, like so many other newcomers, he continues to work at a job that makes very poor use of his training, abilities, and potential. He wistfully sighed and said:

> How could I know the business would never take off, and in fact, that the only thing that would take off was the "businessman" with all my money! I lost everything ... my house, my savings. I couldn't get my old job back and the bills keep coming. Although I was grateful for an opportunity to start fresh here, I spent

so much on the move and the plane tickets. Now I'm driving even more than I ever did on that city bus and for less income!

This was a cautionary tale if I had ever heard one, and I was deeply moved by his candor.

After wishing my driver the best and handing him my card (he later wanted to connect via LinkedIn), I got to thinking what if I could go back in time? What professional advice would I have given him in response to this particular career/ financial gamble? Clearly, he was not fulfilled as a bus driver, so I wouldn't have championed for him to stay in that vocation forever. But what could he have done differently that would have still given him more time with his family and for travel, and to maybe start up his lifelong career passion?

Obviously, I can't turn back time, but I can at least share some thoughts for others who may be facing similar career challenges as newcomers.

Don't believe everything that you've heard. When you're a foreign-trained professional, you don't need to settle for driving a taxi, an Uber, or working in fast food/retail. Instead, try to identify others who got their training outside of your new country and have been successful in the new country. When possible, learn from them.

Sometimes free is too expensive. I have known people who have worked for government-funded career support organizations that provide free services to job seekers who are new to the country. I have also known some newcomers who have received assistance from some of these organizations.

For some newcomers, these services are a perfect fit. For others, however, these services encouraged the newcomers to set their sights far too low … and after spending weeks/months attending workshops and training, they "graduate" to a job for which they are grossly overqualified and underpaid. Part of the problem is that some of these service organizations are staffed by people who are less successful than the people whom they are advising. When the advisor has a very basic post-secondary education themselves (or did not attend a post-secondary institution) and has never been a high earner, they don't always have the insights and nuances about professional life as an engineer, lawyer, physician, etc. that is similar to the frame of reference for their foreign-trained client. In my opinion, the time that certain foreign-trained professionals invest in some of these programs would be better spent pursuing other options and aiming higher. In these situations, the free advice isn't a good match for their training, skills, and potential. Sadly, sometimes the well-intentioned free advice from people who don't understand the foreign-trained professional's situation adequately leads to missed opportunities, expensive mistakes, and unsuitable choices.

Utilize your core skills and abilities in a new way. Credentials and/or job experience acquired before arriving in a new country aren't always recognized or valued the same way they were in your country of origin. So, you may have to reconsider how to use your core skills and abilities in a different role in the new country. This is especially important for employees who have at least ten years of work experience that's aligned with relevant training and education in your country of origin. If you're one of these more "mature" workers, then you should not consider yourself as an "entry-level" person.

Is there a short training program, certification, or partial degree that you can earn that will also give you access to relevant work experience in your new country? Is part of your former training or education eligible for partial credit toward the new training/program?

Is self-employment or starting a small business an option for you – even on a part-time basis? I appreciate that self-employment income can be hard to generate for the first few years so perhaps a more viable option is part-time self-employment while working part-time elsewhere. This really is a bigger topic that could be its own book. I do have plenty of resources on that subject on my blog,[9] and of course, there is even more information online elsewhere.

Consider emerging areas/fields where there are no formally recognized training programs or credentials. By many accounts, many workplaces are at a turning point due to emerging technology and changes in the economy. It's predicted that this will create new opportunities that are linked to blockchain, artificial intelligence, machine learning, green/clean tech, biotech, and others that are still unknown as I write these words. When you're at the cutting edge of some of these fields, the training and credentials are minimal and behind the industry. This makes it easier to be self-taught and become successful based on what you can deliver rather than your certifications.

Find ways to become better integrated into the broader community. Many of the best career opportunities and referral opportunities happen through informal, social, and professional networks. When you're absent from those in person or online conversations, you will miss the best opportunities. Join networking groups that have transitioned into meeting mostly online. Facebook and LinkedIn have thousands of active, busy communities; odds are good that you'll find one for your field.

If you're a student, try the career services office on campus. Career services are typically free and linked to employers who hire and/or provide volunteer opportunities to students. Smart employers love hiring people who started as a co-op or practicum placement since these new employees have already shown their value and suitability while on placement in a temporary role.

Read as much as you can from reputable online publications. Understand how the local workplace functions. Forbes.com and articles on Glassdoor.com and Workopolis.com are good places to start.

Be careful who you listen to. When possible, make sure that the people who are giving you career or business advice have adequate and appropriate training and relevant experience. For employment counsellors and career coaches, the credentials can range from a week-long (or shorter) online training course to a certificate from a community college to a Master's in Social Work or other fields and beyond. Look for recommendations, reviews, and testimonials from previous clients describing that person's service and the results they have generated.

Context matters. Finding an advisor who understands the unique challenges faced by newcomers and/or BIPOC communities is worth the effort.

NOTES

1 White, Martha C. (2014, February 10). 5 Signs You're Overqualified for Your Job. *Time.* https://business.time.com/2014/02/10/5-signs-youre-overqualified-for-your-job/
2 Snee, T. (2020, October 13). Bored at work: Workers who feel overqualified are more likely to look for new jobs. Tippie College of Business. https://tippie.uiowa.edu/news/bored-work-workers-who-feel-overqualified-are-more-likely-look-new-jobs
3 Danielle, B. (2015, May 12). Michelle Obama's "twice as good" speech doesn't cut it with most African Americans. *The Guardian.* www.theguardian.com/commentisfree/2015/may/12/michelle-obama-twice-as-good-african-americans-black-people
4 Usher, A. (2018, May 4). Visible minority numbers rise sharply. HESA. http://higheredstrategy.com/visible-minority-participation-in-university-studies/
5 Sull, D., Sull, C., Cipolli, W., & Brighenti, C. (2022, March 16). Why every leader needs to worry about toxic culture. *MIT Sloan Management Review.* https://sloanreview.mit.edu/article/why-every-leader-needs-to-worry-about-toxic-culture/
6 https://ioadvisory.com/blog/
7 https://ioadvisory.com/blog/
8 https://ioadvisory.com/blog/
9 https://ioadvisory.com/blog/

CHAPTER 3
The Impostor Syndrome

In this chapter, I will explain the basics of impostor syndrome and its consequences. Then, I will give special attention to how the impostor syndrome plays out for people who are part of an underrepresented group – and how to keep it from obstructing one's career progression.

At work, do you ever have the feeling that you don't belong there? I don't mean in the context of fitting-in-with-the-cool-people-by-the-watercooler, but professionally speaking, do you suspect that you don't deserve the position you're in? Do you secretly fear that you don't have the necessary skills? Are you worried that you'll be exposed as a "fraud?" If so, you're not alone. What you are experiencing has been labelled "impostor syndrome." The label sounds dramatic but it's really about feeling undeserving of your achievements, that the success in your life is not real, while also feeling an overwhelming sense of incompetence … even when praised.

This isn't some new "syndrome" to coddle people who are unsure about themselves. Rather, it's a widely recognized problem that affects 60% to 70% of us at some point. It is even experienced by individuals who have achieved significant successes in their life.

Given how common the impostor syndrome is, it's not surprising that many of my clients have acknowledged experiencing it. I have also felt it when I have made big career moves/transitions or taken on certain large contracts – but for a long time I didn't know it had a name.

This is an important topic to address because it's common, but also because it is linked to underemployment. When people let the discomfort of the impostor syndrome prevent them

DOI: 10.4324/9781003328988-4

from seeking and expecting employment that is better aligned with their skills, abilities, and earning potential, it's easy to see how they will be more likely to experience chronic under-employment. The impostor syndrome may also be associated with various forms of bullying and harassment, which we'll address more extensively in subsequent chapters.

THERE'S NOTHING FAKE ABOUT IMPOSTOR SYNDROME

Many high achievers report feeling like intellectual frauds and unworthy of their careers or success. I have encountered professionals who have expressed this unyielding sense of self-doubt and inadequacy when they walk into their work-place. This is equally true for those who have difficulty accepting recognition. The same feelings apply to people who have come into unexpected fame or wealth, or both, and who now feel the only place to land is way down, after a fall from grace.

I recall speaking with a brilliant, award-winning writer from South Africa. Despite having a stellar résumé filled with travel to attend prestigious international writers' festivals, she explained that much of the time she feels like an impos-tor. She described how listening to other writers speak about their success makes her unable to take pride in her own work, and somehow makes her feel like an impostor.

This intrigued me because I've seen the effects that impostor syndrome has had on some of my clients. So, I asked this four-time published novelist, "What about the first time that you learned your book was going to be published internationally – weren't you happy?" Her response was surprising:

> To be honest, the thought I had in my head was that I had fooled them. I even rushed to write another book just to prove I wasn't a fraud. Then, to add to the intense emotions of that accomplishment, I was honored with a very significant award. After the fact, I found out that I was the first Black person ever to receive it. None of this

success changed how phony I felt. I even felt ashamed for rejoicing in any of it.

After talking to this accomplished woman, I wondered why so many ambitious, intelligent, hardworking people experience these feelings. Next, I did what I often do. I did my homework by looking into the research literature and other credible online resources. I confirmed that the impostor syndrome stretches across the spectrum of occupations too. It's a sentiment that's been acknowledged by doctors, teachers, lawyers, athletes, entrepreneurs … and also by artists, actors, photographers, writers, and models. For people experiencing impostor syndrome, the more they achieve, the less genuine it feels and the worse they feel about themselves for enjoying it.

FIVE WAYS TO KNOW IF YOU'RE EXPERIENCING IMPOSTOR SYNDROME

1. You're afraid that you will be found out or fired despite being applauded for good work.
2. You are hesitant to seek further achievements, such as seeking promotions or other exciting opportunities in the workplace. This is true for artists who will not showcase their work or submit their writing for fear it isn't worthy.
3. You experience anxiety and/or embarrassment if/when you speak about your achievements with others.
4. You worry that your accomplishment isn't real or will be taken away.
5. You fear that you got lucky and are not actually qualified for the position or award. Further, you fear that your success was given to you by chance, nepotism, or some other form of favoritism/bias. The fact is that many people get into positions because of nepotism, cronyism, or some other form of favoritism. When they are also qualified, they do not lose sleep over their good luck, they just make the most out of their lucky break. Be like them, savor your opportunity and do your best.

Since this is such a prevalent issue for so many people, here are some ways that you can cope when the impostor syndrome is having a negative impact on you.

COPING WITH THE IMPOSTOR SYNDROME

Recognize the benefits of being a novice. When you are not steeped in the conventional wisdom of a given profession or domain, you can ask questions that haven't been asked before and approach problems in ways that others haven't considered. The outsider perspective is fresh and may allow you to pick up on things that others may miss. Many problems are solved by those from outside the field in question. So, the next time you feel inadequate in a particular field, remember that as an outsider to the role in question, you might have the most critical perspective of all.

Focus more on what you're learning rather than how you're performing. With a learning or growth mindset (rather than a performance mindset), your mistakes are easier to see as an inevitable part of the learning process rather than as more evidence of your underlying failings. In her books, articles, and videos, psychologist Dr. Carol Dweck argues that the growth mindset creates a powerful passion for learning and development:

> In a growth mindset, people believe that their abilities can be developed through hard work and dedication and – brains and talent are just the starting point. This perspective fuels a love of learning and a resilience that is necessary for achieving anything of substance.[1]

When we see ourselves as capable works-in-progress who will continue to improve over time, it's easier to avoid being paralyzed by the impostor syndrome when we are trying challenging new things. We can keep working hard and doing our best while recognizing that we're on a learning curve and getting a little better each day.

Being found incompetent is the number one fear of executives worldwide. So, if you're feeling like an impostor, chances are that other high performers in your situation feel the exact same way.

Based on personal and professional experience, I believe that some special attention is warranted for certain people who are dealing with the impostor syndrome – while also living with the challenges of being some type of outlier. Although characteristics like skin color, religion, sexual orientation, and gender should be on par with eye color when it comes to job performance, there are too many biases at play for these superficial characteristics to be inconsequential.

You may have noticed that most books and articles focus on "traditional" solutions for people who are in the majority. The writers of many career books, career blog posts, and most academic research, are white, able-bodied, cis-gendered, and heterosexual. They choose the topics to pursue and by necessity, they write from their perspective. Sometimes, this leaves BIPOC/BAME readers (and members of other under-represented groups) with less nuanced and relevant advice and information.

Because of my lived experiences and what I see through my work as an executive coach, career coach, and HR consult-ant, I know that the expectations and experiences are differ-ent for people who are "outliers" because of their skin color, religion, and other characteristics. This makes dealing with impostor syndrome even more challenging.

One of the ways this plays out is when you're "the only" or part of a tiny minority. When a woman works in a role where she's in a minority (e.g., in male dominated fields including Science, Technology, Engineering, and Mathematics (STEM)) or when a BIPOC/BAME person works in most corporate environments, they are often the only person who looks like they do.

In January 2019, Sneader and Yee wrote: "One is the Loneliest Number"[2] for the *McKinsey Quarterly*. Sneader and Yee reported several consequences of being "the only" woman in a mostly male work environment. As a Black woman who is usually the only Black person in most rooms, these insights also apply to part of my experience as a racialized person. The analogy is only partially applicable because in many contexts simply being Black is associated with certain unfair realities due to systemic and individual racism.

- Sneader and Yee note that when you're "the only" you may experience extra pressure, anxiety, and a sense of almost being on stage as though if you say or do the wrong thing, negative biases and stereotypes will get reinforced, or prejudices confirmed. They acknowledge that other people who are racialized or "othered" for different aspects of their identity experience far worse.
- Of the women in McKinsey's 2019 *Women in the Workplace* report, 20% said they were commonly the only person of their gender in the room or one of very few. The ratio is much higher in tech and engineering (Huang et al., 2019).
- For women of color, 45% reported being "the only." For men, it was just 7%.
- Being the sole person of color or the only woman in a workplace means being more likely to have their judgment questioned (49%) than women working in a more balanced environment (32%).
- Being the sole person of color means being more likely to be mistaken for someone more junior. So, rather than being recognized at their current level, they are mistaken for someone who is lower down in the hierarchy of power, influence, and rank. Whilst 35% of respondents to Sneader and Yee's survey reported experiencing this, only 15% of Caucasian people surveyed had experienced this.
- Being subjected to unprofessional and demeaning remarks (24% vs 14%).

Sneader and Yee noted that, if "the onlys" are treated this way, it's no wonder they get passed over for promotion.

I would add that if "the onlys" are treated like this, what happens when you compound "only" status with anti-Black racism or anti-Indigenous racism or other types of discrimination? At the time of writing this book, the City of Toronto and the City of Ottawa (the capital city of Canada) had both declared anti-Black racism a public health crisis. Even without those declarations, common sense would predict that any form of discrimination creates a steeper hill to climb. Similarly, over 200 jurisdictions (including New York City) in the United States have made similar declarations.

Limited career progression has been a challenge for most BIPOC/BAME people and finally, following the social justice protests and related conversations that started following the murder of George Floyd in May 2020, most organizations are also acknowledging the problem.

Here are some more nuanced strategies for people who are more likely to be in a minority or even "the only" person like them in their organization or role.

Recognize that you may be underemployed, given your skills, experience, and education. Act accordingly by planning to upgrade your career/role. When others see you in a role that is below your abilities (e.g., you are underemployed) they may assume that your role is consistent with your abilities. What is potentially even worse is that *you* may start to see that your "lower-than-it-should-be-role" is your "real" level. This may tempt you to lower your own internal standards and expectations. Consequently, you may want to consider planning to level up by finding and taking on a role that is a better match for your abilities and education.

Systemic and other forms of racism and discrimination have insidious and pervasive implications that reinforce the impostor syndrome – try not to let racism (or other biases) define you.

Ibram X. Kendi's book *How to Be an Antiracist*[3] makes the point that "racist ideas make BIPOC/BAME people think less of themselves which makes them more vulnerable to racist ideas and behaviors. At the same time, believing racist ideas makes non-racialized/white people think more of themselves. One subtle way that this plays out is that when an organization has a very homogeneous leadership at the director and executive levels, the unwritten and unspoken message is that BIPOC/BAME people are not capable of leadership. The homogeneous leadership team may have unintentionally been created by unconscious biases, but the impact is significant. Recognizing this may help BIPOC/BAME employees and/or members of other equity-seeking groups shake off any lingering doubts they may have about their abilities and their place in the hierarchy.

Know your worth. In my experience, many BIPOC/BAME people are equally if not more qualified than their peers, despite differentials in their employment outcomes. This means that in practice, most BIPOC people don't even get a chance to prove themselves unless they're obviously qualified, despite the dismissive and offensive claims of quotas and tokenism. Sometimes, overcoming the impostor syndrome is as easy as reminding yourself that you've earned your accomplishments and opportunities. Another worthwhile reminder is that non-BIPOC people who get opportunities through their connections and other advantages do not look down on themselves for not "earning" their seat at the table. They accept the chance, and they do not look back or lose any sleep thinking about the people who deserved the role more than they did.

Try not to ruminate or let "head trash" take up too much space. I know this is easier said than done. Some concrete strategies include spending time with people who are at the level you aspire to reach and learning from them. Ideally, these will be mentors or sponsors. Again, I know that often for BIPOC/BAME or other underrepresented people, this is easier said than done. When you do not have access to these people, make use of virtual mentors – watch TedTalks, listen to podcasts, and read/listen to books that will help you gain additional perspectives. One major advantage of filling your mind and spirit this way is that if you find yourself getting negative or ruminating in ways that are not constructive, you can replace this harmful self-talk with content that will help you focus on information that should put you further ahead.

Avoid the trap of believing you need to work twice or three times as hard as others to show your worth. This point is linked to the earlier point about knowing your worth. You may have worked twice or even three times as hard to get to where you are, but now you have probably already proven yourself. Instead of working twice as hard, consider working smarter. If/when possible, try to benefit from the experiences of your peers, others who have more experience than you, and those who are further up the hierarchy. In addition, by not having to "learn the hard way" all the time, you'll save time and likely start to develop more and deeper professional relationships with other successful people.

NOTES

1 Dweck, C. (2015). Carol Dweck revisits the "growth mindset." *Education Week*. www.edweek.org/ew/articles/2015/09/23/carol-dweck-revisits-the-growth-mindset.html?cmp=cpc-goog-ew-growth+mindset&ccid=growth+mindset&ccag=growth+mindset&cckw=%2Bgrowth%20%2Bmindset&cccv=content+ad&gclid=Cj0KEQiAnvfDBRCXrabLl6-6t-0BEiQAW4SRUM7nekFnoTxc675qBMSJycFgwERohguZWVmNDcSUg5gaAk3I8P8HAQ
2 Sneader, K., Yee, L. (2019, January). One is the loneliest number. *McKinsey Quarterly*. www.mckinsey.com/featured-insights/gender-equality/one-is-the-loneliest-number
3 Kendi, I. (2019). *How to be an antiracist*. One World.

CHAPTER 4

Bullying, Harassment, and Discrimination

Unfortunately, bullying, harassment, and various forms of discrimination are common issues that motivate clients to reach out to me. In this chapter, without blaming victims of cruelty, I offer recommendations on how to prevent some of these problems from becoming established so that when employees navigate their way out of these difficult workplace circumstances, they have some strategies in mind to prevent certain problems from recurring. In addition, I share some ideas on how to cope.

The deeply personal experience of being bullied, harassed, or discriminated against at work makes a lot of people want to change jobs because it is such a profoundly negative and disorienting experience. These are not the types of experiences that are easy to "leave at work" at the end of the day – they tend to stick with the victims. In January 2022, Donald Sull, Charles Sull, and Ben Zweig[1] published *Toxic Culture Is Driving the Great Resignation* where they report on an analysis of "34 million online employee profiles to identify U.S. workers who left their employer for any reason (including quitting, retiring, or being laid off) between April and September 2021." Being mistreated at work figured heavily in their findings.

Workplace bullying is unwanted, ongoing aggressiveness that causes psychological and/or physical harm. Workplace bullying creates a psychological power imbalance between the bully and their target(s). Researchers have standardized the criteria for bullying and agree that to count as bullying, it must happen at least once per week for a period of six months, and on average, lasts for a period of two to five years. Bullying causes harm to the victim and any witnesses. The victim experiences trauma first-hand, the

DOI: 10.4324/9781003328988-5

witnesses may experience vicarious trauma. "Research by Employment Background Investigations (EBI) has found being bullied can cause Post-Traumatic Stress Disorder, thoughts of suicide, and suicide itself."[2] When being bullied, harassed, or discriminated against while others within the work environment turn away or actively downplay or deny what's happening (i.e., they gaslight the victim), it can be difficult for the victim to come to terms with what's happening. In this chapter, I'll cover many aspects of bullying, harassment, and discrimination to give you some objective information that you can use to compare against your difficult experiences. Bullying, harassment, and discrimination can undermine the victim's self-confidence and can cause many significant manifestations of physical and emotional stress including nausea, headaches, panic attacks, insomnia, ulcers, high blood pressure, elevated levels of the stress hormone cortisol, etc.

Most adults, but especially parents, aunts, and uncles know that bullying on the schoolyard has been deemed unacceptable. Many schools and school boards have implemented zero-tolerance policies. It's great that someone's looking out for the kids, but what about the "big kids" who experience bullying and/or harassment in the workplace? Most who have experienced workplace bullying or harassment will note that zero-tolerance policies are rarely enforced in the workplace. Instead, typically, the victim ends up leaving while the bully or harasser lives to harm the next unlucky employee who comes along.

Just like with kids, sometimes bullying at work is hidden. But let's face it, adults are often even better at keeping their bad behavior under the radar.

Whether you're an employee who isn't sure if you're imagining that your circumstances meet the criteria for harassment, a manager, business owner, or a colleague who believes in good corporate or organizational citizenship, there are some telltale signs that you can look for to see if there's a problem with bullying and/or harassment within your organization.

The affected employee(s) may be more nervous or anxious around the person who's giving them a hard time. The quality and quantity of the victim's work may be diminished. The victim may become more timid, withdrawn, and sad/depressed. The affected person(s) may be absent more often, especially when they are scheduled to be interacting with the alleged bully. This may even escalate to a claim for short- or long-term disability leave, described as stress leave or burnout.

ORGANIZATIONAL CONSEQUENCES DUE TO BULLYING

Although this book is designed for employees who are trying to make the most of their own careers, from time to time, I share information from the HR/employer perspective as extra context – to support the employee. My rationale is simple – since these situations are so complicated, layered, and disorienting, understanding part of why your employer is behaving in certain ways can be helpful. This is one of those times.

Unfortunately, I have seen organizations where one person has been the root cause of an elevated rate of employee turnover. People had so much trouble dealing with this problematic employee that they routinely sought positions in other parts of the organization so that they could avoid future dealings with the bully, or they escaped from the organization entirely. Sometimes this problematic employee has special skills (e.g., they generate a lot of revenue, or they understand intricate legacy software systems, or they are gatekeepers of sensitive and valuable data, etc.). These special talents, status, or close personal relationships with influential people often protect the bad actor. It's not fair but, when these people have shown troublesome behavior for years and they have never been held to account, you should not believe that you'll be able to change their fate.

In certain organizations, there are times when "everyone" knows and talks about the problem among themselves but not with the management or senior decision makers. Usually, this situation arises when it is commonly known that previous complaints have fallen on deaf ears and that no action was taken to help resolve the problem.

Despite the conventional wisdom on display in so many workplaces, in "The office without a**holes episode"[3] of his WorkLife Podcast, organizational psychologist Dr. Adam Grant notes that

> After decades of working with companies and combing through the research, Stanford's Bob Sutton eventually concluded that assholes make us all less productive. Organizations that don't hire people who treat others like dirt and who call out one another when they act nasty, they're more effective places and they're more humane places to work. In general, in a company, it's better to have a hole than an asshole. So, if there's an asshole, it's really better to just not have the person there. That basically means, don't hire assholes or you should fire assholes.

In other words, even if a bully is high performing in terms of their sales or productivity when you do the final analysis, the lost productivity from the other staff, absenteeism, turnover, and potential legal risks don't come out in favor of keeping that bully. It's too bad more employers and HR folks do not follow the research findings or advice from organizational psychology.

Whenever I am supporting employers who have a problem with bullying or harassment, I like to take them through the facts and highlight the impact that tolerating these counterproductive workplace behaviors has on the bottom line – and people. But, for the most part, it is employees who are living with the consequences of bullying or harassment who seek me out.

There is no doubt that workplace bullying and/or harassment can be a serious problem that requires a thoughtful and strategic solution. It could be due to the personality and/or interpersonal style of the bully (e.g., manipulative, controlling, self-serving, or even narcissistic tendencies). The problem could be due to the bully's exploitation of real or perceived power differentials, or even simple personality clashes. Given the potential complexity of the situation and its consequences, specific, concrete, one-size-fits-all solutions for victims (or management) are not appropriate without knowing the details of the situation. But I do advocate taking some appropriate action rather than ignoring it. The potential mental and physical health implications for the victim(s) are too serious.

I sometimes work with clients who are planning a career change due to bullying and/or harassment that they do not believe will improve. These situations often resemble bad marriages or bad intimate relationships in the sense that the consequences run deep and can be difficult to resolve. There are times when the bullying is so well entrenched and so chronic that it's unlikely that the relationship is salvageable – especially without the cooperation and support of others. In some situations, victims are better off moving on and taking a new job, especially when other interventions have not resolved it. Before moving on and seeking a new position elsewhere, you must ask yourself, does the management/ leadership have the willingness and ability to deal with it in a way that's satisfactory to you? Another good question to ask yourself is, is there an employment lawyer who may be able to offer me some perspective regarding what I should expect in severance or damages if things escalate before I find a new job? Employment lawyers have told me that most people wait too long before seeking independent legal advice. When this happens, the person who has experienced bullying and harassment usually has fewer options available to them. The victim has been "painted into a corner" whereas if they'd sought advice earlier, their lawyer could have preserved additional options for them.

Of course, the ideal situation is to line up a new job before leaving the old one. When that's not possible, then having your financial house in order by having savings and access to affordable credit (e.g., a line of credit) is also a smart condition to satisfy before tendering your resignation.

Most people don't know how to resign from their position without a huge financial loss, or a permanent dent in their resume. Leaving can also be emotionally challenging, provoking anxiety, feelings of (perceived) failure or even guilt depending on how intricate and intimate your work relationships have become. You might try to downplay the severity of the mistreatment you have experienced too. Another concern is finding a new career without relying on your abusive employer as a reference. This can be an intimidating decision, but leaving is critical, just as it usually is for someone who is in a destructive intimate relationship. Other actions to consider include the following:

1. Create a "job exit safety plan." If possible, find at least one ally in the organization who can vouch for you as a reference, perhaps a trusted leader who knows your work reasonably well, a co-worker, customer, or even a client (this depends on your role).
2. Consider people who know you well from volunteer experiences, especially in a leadership or other responsible role. This person may be a good substitute for your lack of a reliable reference from work.
3. Talk to friends, family, or peer contacts who work elsewhere and inquire about leads for other work opportunities.
4. It may be wise to seek out other opportunities in another division or section of the organization, if applicable (especially if you have a generous pension plan and/ or necessary health insurance coverage that you want to retain).
5. If you've only worked under those difficult circumstances for a short period of time and decide to leave, it might be wise to omit the job from your resume and focus your cover letter on illustrating your education and work-related strengths.

THE QUEEN BEE SYNDROME: NOT SWEET LIKE HONEY

Bad behavior in the modern workplace sometimes takes the form of sexual harassment of women by men ... but according to research (and what I've learned through my work), bullying is often garden-variety harassment of women by other women. Bullying done by women to other women is not a topic that gets a lot of attention. This means that when it happens, it can be harder to deal with. Sometimes, with so much attention being placed on gender equality, some women with bad intentions and behavior have gotten a pass and were not held accountable for their dreadful behavior.

Two-thirds of women have been bullied by another woman at work (as reported in August 2018, by Global News[4]). Some of this bad behavior may be related to the "Queen Bee Syndrome" which is well known among teenage girls, as shown in the movie *Mean Girls*. The Queen Bee Syndrome is when a woman in a position of authority sees and treats her subordinates more critically if they are female. Typically, the Queen Bee has succeeded in her career, but refuses to help other women do the same. In fact, sometimes, the Queen Bee will sabotage others to thwart their success.[5] Maybe this is a downside of gender equity, that women are at least as guilty of bad workplace behavior as their male counterparts.

Unfortunately, I've seen evidence of female bullies in businesses, government, and non-profit organizations. It is agonizing to live through as the victim – or to watch it or hear about it after the fact. Whatever the context, workplace bullying, or harassment exists when someone with more privilege and power mistreats someone with less privilege and power on an ongoing basis.

Sometimes there are multiple issues at play. For example, a female bully might be exercising her power over another woman who lacks her stature in the organization but is perceived as a threat because of her experience, reputation, physical appearance, first language, or racial background. The bully denigrates and diminishes the victim so that the victim remains separate from and "less than" the aggressor. This would be most acute when the victim has more education, more years of experience, is harder working, or is physically more attractive.

This bullying or harassing behavior is terrible in its own right. What's even worse is that when people accept and tolerate this type of incivility and workplace bullying/harassment in an organization it spreads and becomes insidious.

Bullying involves psychological and other power imbalances. An initial bullying incident occurs, and for varying reasons, the target/victim does not push back or speak out. Over time, and as long as the target doesn't put up a defense or resist, the bully will continue to push on the target more frequently and more aggressively. Ultimately, an understanding is established whereby the bully has power over the target. The abuse ultimately leaves the target feeling helpless.

I understand that there are many factors that encourage people to keep quiet or look away in the presence of bullying or harassment. For example, this protects the reputations of the victims who do not want to be labeled as troublemakers. In other situations, it is easier for a business owner, leader, or HR person to let the victim give up and leave the organization than it is to reign in the bully/harasser. In other cases, the silence and indifference are mostly about the complicity of the witnesses who could and should have been better allies. Their silence in the face of harassment and the abuse of power is not something to be proud of.

In 2018, the province of Ontario, Canada updated its anti-harassment legislation[6] and it now offers some guidance and relief to the people who are brave and motivated enough to try to make the workplace safer and fairer. Depending on where you live, there may be similar legislation and it's wise to look it up to see where you stand if you're dealing with this in your own work life. At the time this book was being finalized, Title VII of the Civil Rights Act of 1964[7] was the primary federal law that prohibits harassment in the workplace (or in any formal setting) within the United States. This law formally covers most areas of harassment and discrimination in the workplace, with the exception of sexual orientation. The Clear Law Institute[8] notes that

> California, Connecticut, Delaware, Illinois, Maine, New York State, and New York City have passed statutes requiring sexual harassment training, other federal and

state laws, regulations, and court decisions have made clear that employers should provide anti-harassment training to all employees in all states.

Sometimes, bullying is gendered – but in a way that doesn't get much attention. Unfortunately, I have seen situations where a female bully has seemed progressive and talked the talk but didn't walk the walk. For example, a female bully may say things or take positions that make them seem like supporters of gender equality or feminism. For instance, they said the "right" things in response to popular court cases or news headlines, attend annual International Women's Day events, or confess that they have experienced problems associated with the #MeToo movement. It is extremely disappointing to see those women who outwardly speak of being allies who are fighting to end violence against women when in reality they are women perpetrating emotional violence against another woman. It can also be more complicated to hold these women to account because of the mismatch between their words and their actions.

So, in the interest of gender equality, I believe that it's time for men *and* women to consider doing more to create safe, respectful, and inclusive organizations and workplace cultures. Men are not the only ones who should be expected to be good organizational citizens. Women should hold other women to that same standard instead of turning away and pretending not to see what is happening or declining to respond even when they are advised in writing.

SEXUAL HARASSMENT

Sexual harassment continues to be a problem in certain workplaces despite the public and private efforts to thwart it. Typically, when potential clients contact me, if they are dealing with harassment, it's usually non-sexual versions of harassment, bullying, and discrimination. With that said, since I understand that sexual harassment is still happening, I'm including it in this chapter.

Since we spend so much of our waking hours doing our work, we want to assume that the places where we work are safe spaces. On the surface, workplaces often carry a certain level of formality, respectability, and boundaries. Yet, according to research published by the Statistica Research Department[9] in the United States, during a "2017 survey, 42 percent of surveyed women stated they have experienced sexual harassment, while 11 percent of surveyed men stated the same. In total, about 27 percent of American adults stated they have been sexually harassed before." The story is similar in Canada. According to Statistics Canada, based on 2016 data taken from the General Social Survey on Canadians at Work and Home, 19 percent of women had experienced sexual harassment at work in the past year. Unsurprisingly, the situation is no better in Europe. In October 2019, Martin Banks reported on research from April 2019. Among a sample of 5,026 women aged 18 years and over residing in Italy, Spain, France, Germany, and the UK, "six out of ten women in Europe have endured sexist treatment or suffered sexual violence during their careers."

As a woman who specializes in work and business psychology, and who has many years of experience dealing with various career and leadership issues, I recognize that sexual harassment and other abusive behaviors in the workplace are all too common, yet the silence can be deafening.

As with other loaded topics, like politics and religion, many employees and leaders prefer to say nothing, despite the undeniably tense and divisive climate that many victims of harassment/bullying, and BIPOC/BAME, and/or newcomer employees are experiencing. When discussing "taboo" subjects that are linked to religion and/or politics, or sensitive topics like bullying, harassment, and discrimination, consider framing discussions around values which may include the concepts of tolerance, inclusion, human rights, and respect. Values are extremely relevant within the context of willful silence when it comes to racism, sexism, and other behaviors that violate basic norms.

One of the more memorable cases that fueled widespread dialogue on workplace sexual harassment was over 25 years ago. American attorney Anita Hill became an iconic spokeswoman when she bravely came forward with a highly publicized claim against Justice Clarence Thomas, who had been nominated to become a judge for the United States Supreme Court. The details she shared about the gross misconduct and abuse that she experienced while at work was widely challenged and would forever change her life and career (this story is captured in the 2016 film *Confirmation* starring Kerry Washington as Anita Hill). That historical call for action propelled, however slowly, changes in how men conducted themselves with women in the workplace, or at least that is what we had hoped for.

Fast-forward to today and millennials may have never known the face of Anita Hill, the way my peers and I did from watching her televised court appearances so long ago. But there she was in October 2017, speaking once again on camera about the same inequality and abuse of power by men and corporations alike. Had it not been for the date-stamped recent headlines it would be easy to believe that it was still 1991.

Maybe in some ways, we are stuck in the 1990s. How much has been done to stop the apparently rampant abuse via intimidation and control of women in the workplace? Measures to eradicate these problems have been slow, even when a woman is courageous enough to speak out. Many colleagues and other bystanders still seem to remain silent or look the other way.

There has been a promising shift in the way that people are responding to women's claims of abuse. There's less of the *"he said, she said"* debate than we've had to endure with previous high-profile sexual assault situations (e.g., Bill Cosby). In both situations including Weinstein and Cosby, rumors circulated for years about their predatory ways. Yet these men were able to thrive in their professional lives while they continued to assault and/or coerce women with impunity.

In the modern, "post-#MeToo, post-Covid, post-acknowl-edgement of various forms of systemic discrimination work-place," it will likely be easier to deal with sexual harassment than it was in the past. By necessity, most employers are try-ing to be more progressive and understand the importance of psychologically safe and inclusive workplaces.

If you have the wherewithal to confront your abuser, that is probably the most efficient way to shut down sexual har-assment. If your harasser is a classic bully, they may simply back down once you set limits or assert your boundaries. But despite the progress that was made during the #MeToo era, there is also a chance that things could go poorly when you confront your abuser or explain to your employer what is happening.

If you don't have confidence that your abuser will change their behavior or you doubt that your employer will sup-port you following your disclosure of harassment, then you might consider lining up alternative employment. When workplace investigations are launched to look into claims of harassment and other counterproductive behaviors, the process is often so disruptive that the work environment feels tainted to the victim. Those formal processes are set up to determine whether the claims of harassment are founded or unfounded. What often happens in these formal pro-cesses is that people feel obligated to take sides – and some-times people align themselves with the person who seems the most powerful. Typically, this works against the victim. In comparison to all this drama, it's easy to see why finding a new position might be preferable.

I have an aunt who would sometimes say "do you want to be right or do you want to be happy?" In certain cases, involving bullying, harassment, or various forms of dis-crimination, the best course of action is finding a place where you can work in peace even though the "right" thing to do is to hold someone accountable. In my experience, some organizations are extremely toxic, and the leader-ship does not have the appetite to make difficult decisions regarding these sensitive matters. When the writing is on the wall, you are better off taking some personal days and/ or sick days off and spending some time to start your job search elsewhere.

If your employer is sending "the right" messages about workplace health, safety, and wellness then that might be a cue that your employer will treat you with dignity, respect, and confidentiality if you disclose sexual or other harassment. But before you make a disclosure, put your proverbial ducks in a row by confirming that you have someone who will be willing to corroborate your story. Also, make sure that you have notes or other records of what has happened. This documentation should help you seem more credible. If, however, your employer is not especially progressive and you see various types of counterproductive workplace behavior (e.g., discrimination, bullying, harassment, etc.) happening in plain sight, then it suggests that your disclosure may not make much difference. If that is the case, sometimes the remedy is worse than the illness. Or in this context, in the wrong type of organizational climate, the way these sensitive matters are handled feels worse (for victims) than keeping quiet or moving on to a new position. For example, typical workplace investigations force people who are close to the situation to take sides with either the accused or the victim. Often, people feel more comfortable siding with the more powerful accused person since that is the person who will usually stay with the organization following the investigation. Moreover, the more powerful and influential person can also impose consequences or reprisals in ways that the victim rarely can. When potential witnesses chose to remain quiet or side with the accuser it's no wonder that many investigations are inconclusive or decide that the accusations were unfounded. When this happens, it's even more difficult for the victim to feel comfortable or psychologically safe enough to remain in the organization. Despite the progress that some employers have made, there are still some workplaces where disclosing mistreatment may make things worse. Even though getting away with sexual (or other forms of) harassment is unfair, and illegal in some jurisdictions if severe, we still have not gotten to a point where the victims are always protected.

NOTES

1 Sull, D., Sull, C., & Zweig, B. (2022, January 11). *Toxic culture is driving the great resignation*. MIT Sloan Management Review. https://sloanreview.mit.edu/article/toxic-culture-is-driving-the-great-resignation/#article-authors
2 Mattice, C. (2020, July 10). *A closer look: Workplace bullying vs. harassment*. Employment Background Investigations, Inc. www.ebiinc.com/a-closer-look-workplace-bullying-vs-harassment-workplace-violence/
3 Grant, A, (Host), (2019, April 9). The office without A**holes (Season 2, Episode 5) [Audio podcast episode]. In *WorkLife with Adam Grant*. Ted Audio Collective. https://podcasts.apple.com/us/podcast/the-office-without-a-holes/id1346314086?i=1000433927551
4 Racco, M. (2018, August 28). *Two-thirds of women say they've been bullied by another woman in the workplace*. Global News. https://globalnews.ca/news/4411507/women-workplace-bullying/
5 Harvey, C. (2018). When queen bees attack women stop advancing: Recognising and addressing female bullying in the workplace. *Development and Learning in Organizations, 32*(5), 1–4. https://doi.org/10.1108/DLO-04-2018-0048
6 Queen's Printer for Ontario. (2022, March 2). *Preventing workplace violence and workplace harassment*. Ontario.ca. www.ontario.ca/page/preventing-workplace-violence-and-workplace-harassment
7 Universal Class. (n.d.). *Federal law and workplace harassment*. UniversalClass.com. www.universalclass.com/articles/business/federal-law-and-workplace-harassment.htm#:~:text=The%20primary%20federal%20law%20that,Civil%20Rights%20Act%20of%201964.&text=At%20the%20moment%2C%20it%20formally,the%20exception%20of%20sexual%20orientation
8 Johnson, M. (n.d.). *Sexual harassment training essential in all States*. Clear Law Institute. https://clearlawinstitute.com/harassment-training-essential-employees-states-not-just-california-supervisors/
9 Statista Research Department. (2021, March 31). *United States – victims of sexual harassment in 2017, by gender*. [Data set]. Statista. www.statista.com/statistics/787997/share-of-americans-who-have-been-victims-of-sexual-harassment-gender/

CHAPTER 5

Navigating Professional Boundaries

In this chapter, I will share practical tips that most employees can use to establish boundaries linked to how they use their time and interact with others during the course of their work. Often, when I'm helping clients deal with complicated or even toxic interpersonal dynamics at work, one theme that comes up repeatedly is professional boundaries – but most people don't use those words when they are explaining the dilemma. Boundaries are the limits you decide work for you on how people can treat you, how they can behave around you, and what they can expect from you. A simple way to know when someone has violated your boundary is when you feel upset, and you may ruminate about the situation for days or weeks.

In certain work roles such as physician, lawyer, teacher, or therapist, professional boundaries are obvious, but for most of us, there is a lot of grey area. In the aforementioned roles, it's easy to know how to behave – you sign on to a Code of Conduct and rules of engagement when you enter the profession. For others, the rules are less obvious. This is definitely one factor that may be causing a lot of turmoil in the workplace.

Often boundaries are informally set when you start a new job. For instance, the number of hours you'll work, circumstances and conditions of overtime, access to your personal cell phone number, and even issues like whether or not you'll consider dating co-workers.

Some things to keep in mind when setting your professional boundaries include using your values to help you figure out where you'd like to set boundaries. This could mean setting time limits on the number of overtime hours you'll work per week to ensure that you have adequate time for passion

DOI: 10.4324/9781003328988-6

projects and various aspects of self-care (e.g., sleep, exercise, meal preparation, leisure, etc.). Others could include your availability outside of work hours and how you'll deal with work-related emergencies (and what counts as a legitimate emergency).

In 2020, millions of people lived through an applied social psychology experiment that nobody planned for. The workplace literally came into many people's homes. This makes workplace boundaries a more relevant topic than ever – even though most people aren't using the word "boundaries," the construct of boundaries affects most of us.

BLURRED LINES AND WORKPLACE BOUNDARIES

The modern workplace can be complicated – even before the pandemic turned a bunch of things inside out and upside down. Some roles are changing quickly because of automation. Many of us use mobile devices and/or work from home and both of these habits blur the line between work and home. This versatility around how and where we work has many advantages, but it also makes it wise to consider workplace boundaries and some of the consequences of the work–life merge.

I'm a fan of Dr. Adam Grant, another Organizational Psychologist (or Work Psychologist) who is an American university psychology professor and host of *WorkLife*, a terrific podcast that's sponsored by TED, the organizers of all those famous YouTube videos.

In the April 2018, "When work takes over your life"[1] episode of his podcast, Grant describes people who like to blend work and life as integrators. In contrast, segmentors like to keep their work and personal life separate. Segmentors believe that blending work and personal matters is distracting, uncomfortable, and inappropriate. One way to identify a real segmentor is to notice whether they have separate keychains for work and home. Another, more extreme signal is that real segmentors avoid having photos of their family in their office. In general, segmentors report better well-being than integrators do.

In the modern workplace, with 24/7 access to email and remote access to shared drives at work, it's probably becoming harder to be a segmentor since so many workplaces expect ongoing access to employees. This is even more true for people who are working from home. Even for employees who are lucky enough to have a spare room or designated space from which to work from home, the psychological distance between home and work may be too narrow. When an employee is working from their bedroom, kitchen table, or dining room, or they are sharing their workspace with their children or spouse, their work has literally entered their personal space. This is especially hard for segmentors. Segmentors are swimming against the current, since blending or integrating work and life is becoming the norm and the default.

In the past, the natural tendencies and habits of segmentors were probably enough to keep work and life in their preferred compartments. It was easier to separate work from one's personal life. Now, in the modern workplace, segmentors need to be much more intentional about their workplace boundaries if they want things to remain in their proper places.

Some may ask why can't integrators and segmentors just do what makes sense for them. Well, Grant described research that shows that there comes a point where employees' preferences start to affect their overall productivity. So, in practice, a segmentor who can't avoid sharing their work-from-home space with a member of their family – typically, in their family room, kitchen, etc. – will have a hard time. Their circumstances will feel stressful. The distractions and discomfort of never getting away from their work will take a toll on their productivity and their mental health. Consequently, since a business' productivity affects its bottom line, by extension, considering whether someone is an integrator or a segmentor – and what they may need to remain productive – matters.

There are several implications that are tied to working from home while trying to survive a global pandemic – and its long-lasting aftermath. Although there is much to mourn due to the losses that we have taken during the pandemic – and it may take years to regain economic equilibrium – there are some hidden upsides and opportunities.

If you are lucky enough to be able to work from home more regularly, your productivity may have increased – unless you are working from home while also taking responsibility for distance learning for young children. You are no longer forced to listen to the over-sharer in the next cubicle or be endlessly bored by coworkers who don't take social cues.

To be fair, however, those without an ideal home office and young children at home have probably been having a more difficult time staying focused. I would also argue that for people who cared for their children all day without the benefit of school, childcare, camps, or sports, found it to be a tough grind to start their workday after their children went to sleep (or once another adult steps in to take over childcare duties). This scenario was not sustainable for the long term and puts countless working parents at risk for burnout.

CAUTION: WORKPLACE BOUNDARIES ARE NOW MUCH MORE, OR MUCH LESS CLEAR

Working from home can lead to better workplace boundaries, or weakened workplace boundaries (or of course, for certain people, maybe there is no net change).

It can take significant resolve and determination to ignore after-hours messages about work. Ideally, leaders would set the tone and walk the walk, because when senior leaders work around the clock, it puts pressure on staff to reciprocate, but the pay cheque will not necessarily reflect that extra effort.

I generally encourage my clients to set firm boundaries around work, especially now that the lines have become so blurred.

According to research that Dr. Grant cited,[2] our workplace boundaries are affected by physical proximity and time.

Apparently, if you use an electronic device during a class or a meeting, you learn and contribute less – and so do the people sitting near you. Just having your smartphone on your desk reduces your own working memory by 10%, even if your phone is in airplane mode. It also makes you perform 5% worse on an intelligence test. (*I assume that this does not apply when you're chairing a meeting and referring to documents and/or the agenda on the electronic device.*)

This suggests that creating a workplace boundary whereby there are certain meetings that are "unplugged," could result in better attention and fewer interruptions. In fairness, I don't know if these studies are recent enough to track the impact of tablets that are enabled with precise styli (e.g., iPads with the Apple Pencil or the Microsoft Surface Pro with a stylus) that makes it possible to handwrite notes on a digital device.

Research also suggests that it's a good idea to reserve some uninterrupted time for "deep work" so that people can focus on their tasks long enough to reach a state of peak productivity or "flow." This would also reduce the time that's lost following each interruption; it can take 20 minutes to recover and refocus from an interruption. For example, in one firm, after a *Quiet Time* policy was implemented, two-thirds of the employees saw a real boost in their productivity. They designated Tuesdays, Thursdays, and Fridays before noon as a "No Interruptions" time.

France has taken a different approach by legislating a 35-hour workweek to encourage better work–life balance and stronger workplace boundaries. This national law makes it harder for employers to force their employees to work evenings and weekends.

Grant and others argue that leaders need to set the tone and walk the walk. When senior leaders work around the clock, others will assume that's what is required, and they'll also be motivated to work around the clock.

One simple tactic that I recently implemented is helping me respect the personal time boundaries of the team that I work with to ensure that my blog, newsletters, and other deliverables get out on time. Sometimes I need to work evenings or early on Saturday mornings to keep on top of my responsibilities. This often includes sharing information with members of my team. Now that my email software allows me to compose email messages but send them later. I still work some Saturdays, but I can schedule the delivery of those messages for Monday morning. I love the fact that now they do not even need to decide whether or not to look at those messages on the weekend. This feature is available in Gmail and Outlook.

Setting workplace boundaries can be challenging but given the potential impact on productivity and well-being, it is worth the effort ... for employees and employers alike.

OVERSTEPPING WORKPLACE BOUNDARIES

I remember listening to some talk radio and catching the tail end of an interview with a modern-day butler. It was an intriguing glimpse into a profession that not many will ever experience, let alone observe. This butler shared humorous stories and insider secrets about the mastery of his work, but the last bit of his discussion really interested me. He went on to describe a story about a butler who was fired for getting too comfortable with their employer. Although living in his employer's home for several years gave him rare and intimate access to his client's personal life, this did not necessarily mean he could step outside of the distinguished role he was hired for (although it's an easy mistake to make.) And, quite the overstep was made in this story! Apparently, during a formal dinner party, the butler made a sarcastic remark to his boss about minding her calorie count as he was placing the desserts on the table. Evidently, this was a topic they'd joked about in private; nevertheless, this informal banter in front of her guests was an absolute landmine for his career. All at once, the boundary had unwittingly been crossed and the poor butler was gone by the end of the day.

As I switched off the radio program, I got to thinking about how overstepping one's workplace boundaries is a matter that stretches across the borders of most professions. We've all heard the amusing stories about an office Christmas party where someone dips into the punch one too many times and ends up dancing with a Christmas tree, or sloppily flirting with a colleague's spouse. We chuckle about these rumored faux pas, but this can seriously impact one's reputation. But it's possible that violating work boundaries isn't that obvious to some people. I've had clients reveal annoyances about employees not taking social cues such as being inappropriate with others' personal space or constantly interrupting, meddling/interfering in projects and discussions that do not concern them. Similarly, I've cringed listening to an employee overshare a personal/awkward detail about themselves to their superior and thought, "Why on earth would anyone think that's okay?"

I'd like to bridge the gap for those who have made these professional blunders and others who want to avoid making them. I know how easy it is to be confused by work-related situations that seem informal but have unwritten rules. As with the butler story, many people really like their bosses and/or the establishment where they work but sometimes they lose (or forget) their sense of professionalism. Most often this happens when an employee has been in the same environment for years and they feel comfortable there. It's easy to perceive the relationship or organization as a place where they can be relaxed and feel at home. And it's not that surprising since HR and modern businesses foster a welcoming, pleasant atmosphere. For example, many organizations regularly take initiatives to boost workplace morale and employee engagement through company social events. So, it really does become tricky to know where one's professional image begins and ends.

Overstepping boundaries is not always the employee's fault; frequently employers don't provide clear guidelines and/ or conduct themselves professionally. For instance, if your boss tells you a raunchy joke, and then when they ask you how your weekend was, you lightheartedly reply, "Still feeling hung-over!", it's possible that you have stepped over an invisible line, even though you were walking along what you thought was the same track of wit and humor as your boss.

MAINTAINING WORKPLACE BOUNDARIES

Pay attention to your feelings and take notice of other's feelings. When someone's behavior makes you feel uncomfortable, it's a cue that they may be crossing one of your boundaries. The same goes for taking hints around you. If you notice a colleague is busy or overwhelmed, perhaps give them some room to work. Respecting others' space and time is key to staying within professional boundaries.

Setting the right tone in your workplace. Establishing a semi-conservative attitude that is clear and consistent will help establish a solid boundary that others will recognize as your standard. More importantly, this will help everyone stay within those parameters of professionalism.

Calling out workplace bullying and harassment. This includes others not allowing you to express your thoughts, expressing microaggressions, making inappropriate comments, interjecting/interrupting, passive or overtly aggressive body language, taking undue credit for your work, etc. When possible, it's best to address this as it's happening.

When the private becomes public. When posting pictures, events, or comments online consider whether the content is better shared with close friends and family – possibly offline. Many people are liberal about accepting friend requests via social media, but it's easy to forget who is present on your social media feeds. My suggestion is to keep your personal social media persona separate from your professional image and perhaps place privacy settings on your accounts to ensure the two worlds do not collide.

Be nice ... but be smarter. It is wise to remain friendly at work and maintain good peer relationships while also remaining psychologically and emotionally removed from any possible drama or related fallout. This means avoiding office romances, practical jokes, or involving yourself in coworkers' gossip or conflict. This will prevent negative "entanglements" in the workplace while still maintaining effective professional relationships.

Don't procrastinate. It is much more effective to deal with boundary violations promptly; they are easier to explain in the moment than after the fact. With practice, this gets easier. Dealing with these violations in real time may also help prevent further escalations.

PUSH BACK WHEN YOUR BOUNDARY IS CROSSED

My clients have sometimes asked me for ideas about how to push back against unreasonable requests from their leaders and clients because they know that it's an issue hurting their productivity.

Here's a list of phrases and approaches that you might find useful when you find yourself in these situations:

- When asked to do something that seems unreasonable, describe how the request will affect other projects, clients, or your bottom line. Make your rationale relevant to your boss/co-worker/client.
- "If I spend my time on _____, we're going to lose this big client," or "there won't be enough time to do _____."
- "Tell me more about why you need this done."

To deal with unwelcome long, "drop-by" meetings or unscheduled video check-ins:

- Propose that going forward, you set yourselves up for successful and efficient meetings by:
  - creating some structure by preparing a meeting agenda
  - understanding that scheduled meetings can be more efficient, and position you as a professional, especially if someone is treating you as an inferior in some way
  - including an agenda, with start and end times along with topics to discuss
  - proposing a regular check-in to minimize "long and non-productive drop by" visits.

WORKING THROUGH ADDICTION ... WHILE AT WORK

For most of us, even standard professional boundaries – including responding to email during the evenings and weekends – can be difficult to navigate. Other circumstances can get far more complicated. For example, some employees are dealing with sensitive issues like addictions or domestic violence that may be happening outside work hours. These types of personal problems became more prevalent during the pandemic and will have lasting effects. Addictions, intimate partner violence, and other personal challenges may ultimately have an impact on your work performance and/or attendance. In these situations, it can be extremely tough to know what to say to your employer versus what to hold back. As a rule, I think it's wise to say as little as possible upfront and disclose only the essential, high-level basics without sharing all the details. If needed or appropriate, you can share more information later. When you share more information than is needed, you can't take it back. This can be more awkward than it needs to be when it comes to highly sensitive personal information. On the one hand, it is personal, but if/when it's having a negative impact on the professional, then it becomes more relevant for the work context. With the ongoing pandemic and the potentially slow global recovery, this is likely to become a bigger and bigger problem since the rate of substance abuse (and mental health concerns) has risen[3] since the start of the Covid-19 pandemic.

I remember having coffee with a good friend who works in a very different profession than mine. For a little while, we talked shop about our work and traded strategies on how we deal with certain issues. Although she's an accountant and I am a work and business psychologist, we have plenty in common. We both encounter similar problems that our clients are dealing with and these are often issues that most people wouldn't think would come up in our specific lines of work.

The seriousness, prudence, and discretion required to protect our respective clients are often comparable to that of a lawyer or a clinical psychologist, as we all deal with sensitive personal information.

As my accountant friend noted,

> I'm not only dealing with just a client's financial information. I'm also delving into their personal habits and or problems … I have seen lives financially and personally destroyed by addictions, whether it is gambling or substance abuse … often these delicate matters eventually come up.

I reflected on all the times that I've drawn on academic, personal, and professional experiences to help people navigate around complicated life events including mental health issues, harassment, bullying, human rights issues, invisible and visible disabilities, or the fallout from a divorce, separation, or domestic violence.

During this mental exercise, I realized that I have not actually spent any time writing about employees and/or clients that are silently struggling with addiction and its fallout. Drug addiction is also called substance use disorder, and it is defined as a disease that affects a person's brain and behavior and leads to an inability to control the use of a legal or illegal drug or medication. Substances including prescription medication, alcohol, cannabis, and nicotine are considered drugs. When someone becomes addicted, they may continue to use the drug despite the harm it causes physically and mentally, to one's relationships, finances, and workplace performance.

According to Statistics Canada,

> approximately 21.6 percent of Canadians, or about six million people met the criteria for a substance use disorder[4] during their lifetime. Alcohol[5] was the most common substance for which people met the criteria for abuse or dependence at 18.1 percent. More Canadians had symptoms of cannabis abuse or dependence in their lifetime (6.8 percent) compared with other drugs[6] (4.0 percent).

In the United States, the pattern is similar. According to the National Survey on Drug Use and Health[7] (NSDUH), in 2017, "19.7 million American adults (aged 12 and older) battled a substance use disorder." Just as in Canada, alcohol was the most common substance that was abused – "almost 74% of adults suffering from a substance use disorder in 2017 struggled with an alcohol use disorder." The National Institute on Alcohol Abuse and Alcoholism (NIAAA),[8] part of the National Institutes of Health, estimates that approximately 10% of Americans have had a drug use disorder at some time in their lives. The NIAAA also notes that there is under-treatment of alcohol use disorder in the U.S. which may be associated with under-diagnosis.

If 10–20% of people meet the criteria for a substance use disorder, it means that most of us will work with someone who is dealing with an addiction. Despite the prevalence of addictions, it's not a topic that's usually discussed freely in the workplace.

When used long enough and frequently enough, eventually, drugs and/or alcohol can change how our brains work and interfere with our ability to make choices, leading to intense cravings and compulsive use. People who have become addicted or dependent on drugs or alcohol often experience:

- problems with their memory
- impaired judgement, attention, and decision making
- impulsiveness
- loss of self-control
- and depending on the substance, paranoia, aggressiveness, hallucinations, and a higher risk of unintentional injuries, accidents, and domestic violence incidents (e.g., alcohol and drugs are partly to blame in an estimated 80%[9] of offences leading to jail time in the U.S. These incidents include domestic violence, driving while intoxicated and offences related to damaged property).

The symptoms associated with addictions can make good performance at work (and daily living) more difficult. Obviously, inappropriate behavior, unstable moods, and impaired judgment/attention/memory make it hard to bring one's best self to work. When what's happening outside of work is having a profound negative impact on your ability to perform effectively at work, it may be time to consider checking in with your family doctor and/or explaining what's happening to your employer. If you have a reasonable relationship with your boss or direct supervisor then that's probably a smart place to start to explain that you've been experiencing a personal issue that you are resolving. If you do not have that type of relationship with your direct supervisor, consider checking your employee handbook or consulting with your union or employee assistance program (EAP) to map out a more appropriate first step.

What happens in our personal lives can have a profound effect on our professional lives. Problems can escalate quickly when someone is dealing with something as complex and all-consuming as an addiction. When someone is in recovery from an addiction, they will probably identify with the notion that maintaining their sobriety while also making meaningful progress in their professional life feels like more effort than they may be comfortable taking on. The metaphor of planes taking off against the wind that I shared at the outset of this book feels relevant and timely. The key takeaway here is that common obstacles feel significant and can make it *seem* like there's no way forward to a better work situation. But, just as a plane can take off against the wind, motivated people with the right systems, support, and tools, in place can safely launch or relaunch their careers.

Boundary issues also can impact your career progression when a boundary violation results in you overworking in a manner that leaves you depleted and unable to perform as effectively as you are capable of. Boundary violations caused when others exaggerate or create power differentials can erode your self-image and self-confidence. These workplace bullying dynamics can start with minor boundary violations and escalate into something more severe and with dire mental health consequences. One example of a minor boundary violation is when someone offers a backhanded compliment that makes you feel uncomfortable. It's potentially minor because there's a chance that there was no bad intent. If you say, something like "hmmm … I'm not sure how to interpret your compliment" it puts the person on notice that you heard it, probably didn't like it, and you're calling them on it. It gives the person a chance to offer a more sincere and unambiguous compliment if that was their intention. If it was intended to hurt, the person might try to gaslight you and say something about not being so sensitive. Once bullying sets in and you're more focused on survival than thriving and delivering your best work, your career can stall. Much of your mental and emotional energy will be drained by self-protection rather than high performance. This in turn can leave you underemployed, not realizing your potential, and losing out on the income that you should be earning.

NOTES

1 Grant, A. (Host), (2018, April). When work takes over your life (Season 1, Episode 8) [Audio podcast episode]. In *WorkLife with Adam Grant*. Ted Audio Collective. https://podcasts.apple.com/us/podcast/the-office-without-a-holes/id1346314086?i=1000433927551

2 Grant, A. (Host), (2018, April). When work takes over your life (Season 1, Episode 8) [Audio podcast episode]. In *WorkLife with Adam Grant*. Ted Audio Collective. https://podcasts.apple.com/us/podcast/the-office-without-a-holes/id1346314086?i=1000433927551

3 Rodriguez, T. (2021, August 5). *Covid-19's continuing toll: Increasing alcohol use and liver disease disproportionately affect women. Psychiatry Advisor.* www.psychiatryadvisor.com/home/topics/addiction/alcohol-related-disorders/covid-19-pandemic-disproportionate-affect-on-women-led-to-increased-alcohol-use/

4 Pearson, C., Ali, J., & Janz, T. (2015, November 27). *Mental and substance use disorders in Canada* (No. 82-624-X). Statistics Canada www150.statcan.gc.ca/n1/pub/82-624-x/2013001/article/11855-eng.htm

5 Pearson, C., Ali, J., & Janz, T. (2015, November 27). *Mental and substance use disorders in Canada* (No. 82-624-X). Statistics Canada www150.statcan.gc.ca/n1/pub/82-624-x/2013001/article/11855-eng.htm

6 Pearson, C., Ali, J., & Janz, T. (2015, November 27). *Mental and substance use disorders in Canada* (No. 82-624-X). Statistics Canada www150.statcan.gc.ca/n1/pub/82-624-x/2013001/article/11855-eng.htm

7 American Addiction Centers. (2022, March 11). *Drug & substance abuse addiction statistics*. American Addiction Centers. https://americanaddictioncenters.org/rehab-guide/addiction-statistics

8 U.S. Department of Health and Human Services. (2015, November 18). *10 percent of US adults have drug use disorder at some point in their lives*. National Institutes of Health. www.nih.gov/news-events/news-releases/10-percent-us-adults-have-drug-use-disorder-some-point-their-lives

9 Gateway Foundation. (n.d.). *The effects of alcohol abuse & addiction*. Gateway Foundation. www.gatewayfoundation.org/about-gateway-foundation/faqs/effects-of-alcohol-addiction/

CHAPTER 6
Toxic Workplaces

One of the most common reasons people reach out to me is because they are uncomfortable in their current workplace. A boss or colleague is making their lives hell or, due to unwritten rules, they sense no clear path to success within their organization – despite excellent performance. Simply put, their workplace is toxic. In this chapter, I'll describe some of the common ways that workplaces can be toxic. This chapter is important because often when someone is in a toxic work environment, others may be motivated to downplay how bad it is … which can add to the disorientation that one might feel while emersed in a toxic workplace. In other words, when you read descriptions of toxic workplaces, you can use those descriptions as criteria to help you evaluate your own situation. I will also summarize some of the root causes of workplace toxicity and provide some suggestions for further reading. Where appropriate, I will describe the impact of a toxic workplace on individuals who are suffering – and their careers. Finally, I will share some strategies for surviving these environments.

The issue of toxic workplaces is probably more complicated than it looks. Usually, the work environment is awful because of the behavior of others – but the bad behavior is often covert rather than obvious and transparent. There is active manipulation to keep the dirty tricks and cruelty under the radar. And in some cases, the victim employee is subject to gaslighting (i.e., the use of psychological techniques to manipulate someone into questioning the validity of their interpretation of their circumstances or even their own sanity) combined with witnesses who look the other way.

The situation is also complicated because the person struggling within the toxic environment's livelihood is at stake

 DOI: 10.4324/9781003328988-7

and, in the interest of self-preservation, they want to move on to a new workplace without triggering even more bitterness and/or revenge. When creating a graceful exit from this type of situation, it can be difficult then to get references from the former employer. Also, there are times when the bosses or colleagues do not want the victim to leave because the victim is doing excellent work that will go undone should s/he leave.

I wrote this chapter to offer some understanding of the reasons that toxic situations happen in the first place. The reasons that I'll address include flawed hiring practices, poor leadership, and some of the roles where toxicity may be most common. Spending time on hiring practices may seem strange for a book designed to help people improve their careers, but my belief is that when you understand some of the hiring practices that enable toxic workplaces, you will be better positioned to avoid taking jobs where these red flags are visible while you are going through the hiring process. Similarly, when you understand some of the workplace roles where these problems are more prevalent, then you may be able to avoid working in those contexts or at least navigate them differently.

CHARACTERISTICS OF TOXIC WORKPLACES

Any online search using the keywords "toxic workplace" will turn up countless pages of links yet there's no solid consensus on what constitutes a toxic workplace. In March 2022, Sull, Sull, Cipolli, and Brighenti published *Why Every Leader Needs to Worry About Toxic Culture*.[1] They studied the negative comments from over 1.3 million Glassdoor reviews from U.S. employees who worked in a sample of large organizations from 40 industries (namely the Culture 500). They distilled their findings into the "Toxic Five" – the attributes that taint and poison the corporate culture. The toxic five include disrespectful, noninclusive, unethical, cut-throat, and abusive behaviors. The toxic five elements have the largest impact on how employees evaluate their corporate culture and contributed most to the first six months of the Great Recession, during which 24 million American employees left their job. Although Sull, Sull, Cipolli, and Brighenti's work focused on the private sector, in my experience supporting clients who work in the public and non-profit sectors, much of their work seems to generalize.

To be sure that we all remain on the same page, I'll go into more detail on the toxic five. Sull, Sull, Cipolli, and Brighenti (2022)[2] defined disrespectful workplace behavior as a lack of courtesy, consideration, and dignity for others. Noninclusive behavior included inequity or unfairness for members of the LGBTQ2+ communities, people with disabilities, racial inequity, age and gender inequity, and a cluster of behaviors that include favoritism, cronyism, and nepotism. Unethical behavior encompasses dishonesty and a lack of compliance with regulations. Cut-throat behavior includes ruthless internal competition and backstabbing. Finally, abusive behavior includes bullying, harassment, and general hostility. It's no wonder this was a powerful force triggering employee turnover en masse.

OTHER CONDITIONS ASSOCIATED WITH TOXIC WORKPLACES

Next, I will discuss two root causes of toxic corporate work cultures that I've seen during my time as an HR consultant, career coach, and executive coach: Poor leadership and problematic hiring practices.

Most employers and their leaders appreciate that they are responsible for creating a workplace that respects and protects employees' health and safety. When a municipal health unit gives a restaurant or other workplace a low grade, people know that it's risky there – you might get sick or hurt. If an organization's culture perpetuates harm for certain employees, shouldn't there be a warning to others so that they know to avoid or at least proceed with extreme caution? Imagine if workplace audits and danger signs were more common? What does a harmful work environment say about the organization's leadership? Simply put, I believe that when employees are (chronically) physically or emotionally/psychologically hurt at work, by bullying, harassment, or any form of discrimination it demonstrates a lack of effective leadership. I appreciate that some leaders believe that their primary responsibility is to protect profitability, productivity, and related metrics. I can't argue that those targets are not important – but I will also argue that ignoring the oppression and harm that employees are suffering from has a moral and a practical imperative. We will return to a fuller discussion on inclusive leadership that supports all, not only some employees, in the next chapter, "Identity Is Complex."

POOR HIRING PRACTICES INVITE WOLVES INTO THE WORKPLACE

When it comes to people getting ahead professionally in the proverbial "work jungle," most of us have heard or used descriptions that come from the animal kingdom, including:

- "Wow, Mark in sales is a real tiger."
- "You don't want to mess with that lawyer, she's a real shark when it comes to litigation."
- "Have you met the new guy from accounting? He works like a dog to get the job done."

Clearly, there is no shortage of animal characteristics to describe a person hard at work. But what about the more predatory traits that are found in the wild? Does having a knack for sniffing out the weak, and skill for fearlessly tracking and prowling one's target really pay off in the work place? Apparently, it does, but not always with the best outcomes for *all* parties involved.

This got me thinking about a 2006 book titled, *Snakes in Suits*[3] by Dr. Paul Babiak and Dr. Robert D. Hare, which examines psychopaths and how they rise to the top by slithering up the corporate ladder. The book's focus is not on the more popularly accepted ideologies of psychopathy, which is often aligned with horrific crimes. Instead, this book is about how certain *corporate* or workplace psychopaths hone their skills in the professional realm with an insatiable need to attain influence, power, and control over the people and companies they work for ... while making money.

Paraphrased from the book jacket:

> Researchers Dr. Babiak and Dr. Hare have long studied psychopaths. Dr. Hare, the author of *Without Conscience*, is a world-renowned expert on psychopathy, and Dr. Babiak is an Industrial/Organizational Psychologist. Recently the two came together to study how psychopaths operate in corporations, and the results were surprising. They found that it's exactly the modern, open, more flexible corporate world, in which high risks can equal high profits, that attracts corporate psychopaths. They may enter as rising stars and corporate saviors, but all too soon they're abusing the trust of colleagues, manipulating supervisors, and leaving the workplace in shambles.

The official terminology for this pattern of behavior is Antisocial Personality Disorder (ASPD or APD), a personality disorder characterized by a long-term pattern of disregard for, or violation of, the rights of others. A low moral sense or conscience is often apparent, as well as a history of crime, legal problems, or impulsive and aggressive behavior.

Just because someone meets the criteria for ASPD or APD does not mean they will become a twisted killer as personified in films such as *American Psycho*. In fact, the one accurate aspect of *American Psycho* is not that Patrick Bateman is an axe-wielding serial killer by night ... but rather who he is professionally by day. He is well groomed, intelligent, structured, and as meticulous as he is ambitious in everything he does, as well as calculating enough to feign a suitable amount of sociability and good humor despite maintaining a spirit of intimidation. Statistically speaking, most people with this disorder do not usually grow up to be murderous thieves – instead, they develop into respected members of their community. They manage to have a gift for polishing their personas and are usually successful. More importantly, they often go their entire lives undiagnosed as being a corporate psychopath. Behind closed doors, however, in their personal lives, things may be different. The spouses of these corporate psychopaths may live quiet lives full of turmoil and struggle as described by Martha Stout in her 2005 book *The Sociopath Next Door*.[4]

Now, borrowing again from the animal narrative, I would argue that corporate psychopaths are not so much slinking and slithering throughout certain organizations as they are portrayed in *Snakes in Suits*, but more cunning like a wolf. I prefer the wolf analogy because there is a duplicitous nature about them. Most of us will immediately recoil from spotting a snake – instinctively sensing its potential to strike. But a wolf can represent many appealing qualities, some that mimic the traits of a friendly, trustworthy pet … but also have the capability to randomly turn aggressive.

With my coaching clients, I have repeatedly dealt with the fallout associated with toxic workplaces and many of the negative consequences come from a less obvious source. It can take a significant amount of time for these "wolves" to reveal their true intentions, and even after being discovered, they are usually skilled at maintaining their positions of power through bullying and other forms of manipulation and/or exploitation.

It is not surprising to me that a wolf is hard to spot in the workplace. This may be due, in part, to the fact that they have been the ones with the most admirable boss-like characteristics, and all too frequently are placed in positions of authority. For example, being methodical, determined, bold, assertive, and visibly refined are things we look for in a leader or in upper management and the executive ranks. But those very same attributes are also found in people who usually are only invested in themselves and don't care so much about the people whom they work with.

For employers and leaders, the end goal should be healthy employee morale, good productivity, and company growth, yet most people with these wolf-like personality traits tend to focus on the financial/status benefits that affect them personally, not collectively. They also have little to no loyalty, and once they feel threatened, vulnerable, or slighted, they can exact a great deal of harm to an individual or employer/organization.

Another flaw found in these wolf-like people is their ruthless competitive nature. Often resorting to unkind methods that include intimidating, belittling, manipulating, and slandering fellow co-workers … as well as criticizing and insulting people behind closed doors with no remorse. Sadly, those who fall victim to these tactics usually leave the organization and the wolf continues to prowl further ahead within the organization with even less competition.

These "corporate wolves" are most likely reaching higher levels within organizations than those who do not possess these cut-throat behaviors. The presence of corporate wolves becomes a matter of company culture rather than an isolated issue when these wolves' bad behavior is accepted, and their victims are left to fend for themselves or leave.

Unintentionally, many well-meaning organizations and businesses select these corporate psychopaths because they appear to fit the bill, at least superficially, when it comes to being clever, in charge, and fiercely preoccupied with being the best … but at what cost?

THE FOX AND THE WOLF: HOW WOLVES ENTER THE WORKPLACE

Many of us remember hearing the story of Little Red Riding Hood when we were kids. This cautionary fairytale was not told exclusively for our entertainment, it was designed to warn children to be leery of strangers who may lure and prey upon them through disguise and false kindness. As we got older, we probably became familiar with the popular saying, "beware of a wolf in sheep's clothing," which has been used frequently and ranges from biblical passages to the legendary *Aesop's Fables*. The messaging throughout seems to be consistent and captures the sentiment that not all who appear harmless are, and that underneath the veneer of a welcoming grin can sometimes await a dangerous bite.

Some workplaces are almost like a natural habitat for corporate wolves … so it is not the employees' fault when they end up in a wolves' sights or crosshairs. Most people don't know much about "corporate psychopaths." Another hidden problem is that most HR people and business owners believe that they have a real knack for hiring great people. They count on being able to spot great candidates without worrying about time-consuming or seemingly tedious standardized hiring processes or tools. In my opinion, however, the prevalence of awful workplace cultures suggests that the favored hiring processes are contributing to bad hires and broken, unhealthy, corporate cultures where chronic harm is done.

Over the years, and especially while supporting clients, I have explored the presence and impact of these deceitful people who act like wolves or professional predators in the workplace. I have seen directly and second-hand through clients' experiences how these proverbial wolves are probably "corporate psychopaths," who often become successful and powerful in upper management and executive roles by using their skills in exploitation, manipulation, and other abusive methods to get ahead. Based on experience and while doing research to find solutions for my clients' situations, I have identified a few ways businesses and other organizations can prevent these types of predators from roaming their halls.

It is important that employers are aware that often these types of "wolves" never stop hunting to get to the top. One potential telltale sign is someone who appears to be significantly more motivated and competitive than other employees *and* is willing to cross lines and boundaries that "regular" people won't cross to get what they want.

To be fair, an overly ambitious employee is not always a corporate psychopath. But assessing someone's high ambition, along with *how* they attain promotions, accolades, and influence, is a good place to start.

As noted above, in *Snakes in Suits* by Drs. Babiak and Hare, due to their controlling and selfish nature, corporate psychopaths are instinctively drawn to positions that give them power and control, as well as occupations that provide wealth and high status.

Clearly, the best way to avoid the damage that these corporate psychopaths/wolves can cause is to avoid hiring them in the first place. Once you let one in, the harm and destruction to staff and eventually a business' reputation and bottom line can be almost immediate.

To borrow from the animal narrative again, in my role as an HR Consultant who has supported employers, I recommend that employers think like a clever fox when potentially dealing with a corporate wolf. Below, I present four ways to increase the odds of spotting a wolf early – especially if you're able to participate in any hiring or promotion processes and/or decisions that could have a significant impact on your workplace climate.

BEWARE OF THE HALO EFFECT

The halo effect is a type of cognitive/thinking bias where our general impression of a person influences how we feel and think about his or her character. Essentially, your overall impression of a person ("He is so charming and charismatic!") influences your evaluations of that person's specific traits ("He is also smart!"). A related issue is that the halo effect may cause us to assume that someone is also an overall good person. Watch for this common mistake if you're involved in a hiring or promotion decision so that you don't create unpleasant consequences. Carefully constructed reference checks are a good place to probe for a candidate's character and potential unsavory behavior.

SOMETIMES A CORPORATE WOLF CAN BE AS HARD TO SPOT AS SALT IN WATER

Many of the qualities associated with corporate psychopaths are also on the "wish list" of most employers. For example, which employer isn't impressed when a job candidate is articulate, intelligent, and self-confident? When seen from a different perspective, they may also have a grandiose sense of self-worth. From another angle, when a candidate seems strategic, they may also be calculating. There is nothing wrong with these qualities. It is more a matter of confirming that the candidate doesn't also have a dark side that shows up often and hurts a lot of people. Consider revisiting your interview and reference checking steps so that you are more likely to notice a lack of empathy, humility, or a core of ruthlessness, even toward colleagues who are supposed to be on the wolf's team.

DO CERTAIN OCCUPATIONS AND INDUSTRIES ATTRACT CORPORATE PSYCHOPATHS?

If you think about some of the extremely popular crimes and scandals that have happened in workplaces and have been documented by the mainstream traditional and social media, you will see that they line up with many of the fields and roles below where corporate psychopaths are over-represented. For example, the 1990s Bre-X mining scandal where, after widespread reports that Bre-X had found a gold mine in Indonesia, the stories told by the founder and his confederates/co-conspirators were found to be fraudulent. The 2001 $63.4 billion Enron scandal is another vivid example whereby several directors and executives fraudulently hid large losses in Enron's projects. Ultimately, some of the leaders involved were sentenced to prison. Deeply troubling and unsavory sexual misconduct among many Catholic priests is another graphic example. Countless problems related to excessive force, abuse of power, racial profiling, and murder are associated with police in the United States (e.g., the high-profile cases involving Trayvon Martin,

Ahmaud Arbery, Breonna Taylor, George Floyd, and others) and Canada (e.g., a 2022 report[5] that acknowledges that Black residents in Toronto are 20 times more likely to be killed by police than other residents, even though they represent a minority within the city). When hiring for certain roles or in certain fields listed below, it can be even harder than it looks to find people who have all the right qualities but don't also have the more sinister qualities associated with corporate psychopaths. Here is a short list, from Drs. Babiak and Hare where corporate psychopaths seem to be overrepresented:

- Television/Radio
- Sales
- Law
- Policing
- CEO/Executives
- Surgeons
- Journalists
- Clergy
- Chefs
- Civil servants.

Most of us know the expression that some people/things are "too good to be true" so we should be extra cautious since there's a good chance that something is wrong or bad. Here are some red flags that when taken with other cues, may be a good sign to dig a little deeper while going through the hiring process:

- Too much flattery of the interviewer(s)/company.
- Extreme confidence bordering on arrogance during the hiring process.
- Acting as if the hiring process is a formality and that they are entitled to the role.
- Too assertive during the interview/hiring process.
- The applicant's past work history doesn't quite make sense or inspire confidence (e.g., how long do they stay in jobs? How do they describe past colleagues/employers? Something seems "off" regarding their references … their references seem to be extremely careful about how they describe the candidate, there are significant pauses

as they choose their words and qualify their comments, for example, "from what I have seen first hand, Chad is _____" rather than "Chad is well-liked, he seems to have really strong and warm relationships with his peers, direct reports, senior leaders, and clients.").

When hiring people who will work in a leadership capacity and/or have significant influence, it is worth taking the extra time and effort that it warrants to get it right. The consequences of letting a wolf run wild at work can be dire.

THE PROFOUND IMPACT OF TOXIC WORKPLACE CULTURE ON PEOPLE AND THEIR CAREERS

In the United States, "between April and September 2021, more than 24 million American employees left their job." This phenomenon has been labeled the Big Quit, the Turnover Tsunami, and the Great Resignation. In January 2022, Sull, Sull, and Zweig published a research article about how *Toxic Culture Is Driving the Great Resignation*.[6] They note that "more than 40% of all employees were thinking about leaving their jobs at the beginning of 2021." Sull, Sull, and Zweig analyzed the content of 34 million online employee profiles to identify American employees who quit their job for any reason between April and September 2021. As expected, companies with healthy workplace cultures had lower turnover during the first six months of the Great Resignation. Interestingly, they discovered that a toxic workplace culture is 10.4 times more powerful than compensation in predicting employee turnover.

Sull, Sull, and Zweig 2022 noted that "the leading factors that contributed to toxic culture include a failure to promote diversity, equity, and inclusion; workers feeling disrespected; and unethical behaviour." In March 2022, Sull, Sull, Cipolli, and Brighenti followed up with a deeper dive article on workplace culture – "Why Every Leader Needs to Worry About Toxic Culture."[7] Their goal was to help leaders understand and then address the issues that cause employee disengagement and turnover. The 2019 Society for Human Resource Management (SHRM) report "The High Cost of a Toxic Workplace Culture – How Culture Impacts the Workforce – and the Bottom Line"[8] estimates that employee turnover triggered by a toxic culture cost U.S. employers nearly $50 billion per year before the start of the Great Resignation. Clearly, this is a lose–lose proposition for employees and employers alike. As a rule, people do not quit jobs lightly – it's a big decision since one's livelihood is at stake.

In this next section, I'll share some strategies for navigating toxic workplaces – starting with some ideas about how to avoid them in the first place.

RED FLAGS TO WATCH FOR DURING THE INTERVIEW AND HIRING PROCESS

A client booked an appointment for some coaching after wasting her time on one too many interviews that just felt wrong. She wanted to know if she was just being too sensitive and cautious about the unusual hiring processes or if this is the way things are these days? Fundamentally, she was concerned about red flags during the hiring process that might be signals that the corporate culture might be toxic or unpleasant in some way.

She described her experience:

> I went for an interview for a management position that started off absolutely wrong. To begin with, the manager interviewing me had no idea who I was. She started off the interview by saying, "So I haven't had a chance to read your resume. You have an HR background, right? Why did you leave your last job?" It was an awkward start, because I hadn't actually left my job, and no, I'd never worked in HR. I felt disrespected right off the bat. I'd put a lot of effort into preparing. I'd sent this company a carefully crafted cover letter and a targeted resume that highlighted my most relevant employment. I'd invested in a new suit, and

I'd rehearsed for hours how I would answer the typical interview questions. Twenty minutes in, I was thanking them for their time and heading for the door.

I would say no, she was not too sensitive. It is a red flag when a prospective employer does not give you the attention, time, or respect that you deserve during the interview process.

A related red flag is when you do not get to meet the person to whom you'll be reporting. Most people who care about their work also care about who joins their team. They will want to participate in the hiring process, even if only as observers.

First interviews may be with HR for general screening purposes, and they are often done by phone or video. If you go to a second interview and the boss to whom you would be reporting is not present, and never shows up to meet you (without any explanation) you may be walking into a hornet's nest. Either there is a high turnover rate, or the position is not important enough to warrant their attention. Worst of all, the boss is possibly being left out of the hiring process altogether – talk about a red flag!

Often, when we are looking for a new job, we really want to make sure that we are chosen by the potential employer. We may be motivated by a deep desire to pay off student debt, the need to provide for ourselves and our loved ones, and for the security that comes from having a steady paycheck. However, we should also be evaluating a potential employer for their qualities.

After finding oneself in a bad workplace, most people are determined to avoid making that mistake a second time. Now that I have passed the 20-year mark since finishing university, I have the benefit of 20/20 hindsight from a lot of work experience – plus some of my clients' experiences. Here are some red flags to watch for so that you can spot a bad workplace before accepting a letter of offer. They are situations related to the hiring process which I have seen personally or indirectly but up-close.

Noticeably High Turnover
If a job really is terrific then people should not be motivated to leave, repeatedly. If an organization is always recruiting, yet never growing, it is a bad sign. It could mean that there is poor management, a lack of opportunity for advancement, a bad workplace culture, less-than-competitive pay, or something even more sinister like a culture of harassment and/or discrimination. If you see this company constantly advertising the same job opening, take note, and apply with caution.

An Endless Hiring Process
This one is tricky. Some organizations recognize that finding the right employee for a specific role may take a while. But in some cases, a long, drawn-out, tedious hiring process implies that they don't really know what they are looking for. Then, even when they have reams of information about a job candidate, they are scared to decide.

Working in an organization where the leaders are driven by fear and are reluctant to make decisions can be an incredibly frustrating existence. Fear of taking well-managed calculated risks to the point of paralysis is something that can permeate a workplace. If that is not your thing, you may have an extremely hard time working in that type of environment.

No Explanation About Why the Position Is Open
When a position becomes available because an organization is growing or pivoting into a new area then the owners/leaders are normally happy to talk about it. These changes imply a forward momentum and progress. These developments are all easy to explain, and all make sense. When an organization is unenthusiastic about explaining why a position is available or they just beat around the bush, it may suggest that there is a problem. It could be that nobody can stand working with someone who has been in a particular role for a long time – so there's a revolving door around that person. It could even point to a serious problem like workplace bullying or harassment.

The Interview Feels Too Easy

If your interview feels too easy, it could be a red flag. A serious interviewer looking to hire a professional candidate will want to test your mettle with some hard questions. If you walk away thinking "that was too easy," it can be a sign of high turnover, and that they are looking for a warm body and almost any warm body will do.

The Company Isn't "Selling Itself" to You

For most organizations, a job interview is still a formal affair. Be wary of a prospective employer who seems a little too casual about your time. Red flags are he, she, or they being late for the interview, or repeatedly checking their email, texting, constant interruptions, and an overall sense that this person is generally not fully focused on the interview.

THE WORKPLACE BAIT-AND-SWITCH

For years, I have worked with Melissa, a creative writer of novels and poetry, who helps me out by proofreading/copyediting my blogs and suggesting potential topics. She mentioned the fact that some of her friends had experienced what sounded like the "bait and switch" scenario – but in the workplace. I did some research, and this chapter was born. When I've shared this topic via social media or on my blog, I know that it has struck a nerve because quite a few people have sent emails or called me to discuss their own workplace bait-and-switch situations. There is no doubt that in most of these situations, it is a switch from something desirable to something undesirable ... and often toxic.

Some of my clients have endured the unfortunate circumstance of having been lured into accepting a promising job that ended up being entirely different – in a bad way – once they started. It is a common concept that cuts across domains.

Bait-and-switch originally described retail companies using false or misleading advertising to draw in customers with an attractive offering. Once customers are on-site, the great deal they came in for is no longer available – but more expensive alternatives are available. The unsuspecting shopper shifts their attention to what is within easy reach and a sale is made.

Misleading or false advertising in the commercial domain is not uncommon. But bait-and-switch also happens in some workplaces. Sometimes the job described in a job posting and even during an interview turns out to be different than the actual job that is offered.

I have a close friend who told me about working part-time as a server while she was a university student. She said that sometimes those waitressing jobs include acting as a hostess, bartender, or busser, and the undesirable task of cleaning the kitchen and bathrooms after closing time. While those specific duties were not advertised or mentioned in the job interview, it was assumed by her employers to be part of her job.

Over the past few years, I have heard similar stories from clients who described professional roles and work assignments that have been quite different from what they had expected based on what was advertised. As a rule, we only think about this when the job we end up with is worse than the job that we thought we were accepting. The present discussion does not apply to the happy circumstance of taking a job and realizing it was different but far better than we expected.

One client said, "I joined a new accounting firm with the promise of a range of desirable clients to work with, but instead I ended doing payroll for the company and given almost no other tasks."

In my role as a career coach, I see this as a failure of an organization's HR policies. It is clearly a bait-and-switch tactic to unload unappealing grunt work, undesirable work hours, or an unreasonable workload on a new employee, hoping they will not notice or make any waves because they are new to the organization and don't know any better. Anecdotally, it is hard to see how the bait-and-switch is the only negative aspect of an organization. Poor HR policies, a reputation for misleading prospective employees, and unsustainable work-loads seem to go hand-in-hand with other aspects of toxic workplaces (e.g., complicity in the face of ongoing bullying and harassment).

It is truly insidious because the employer's deceptive strategies are often tolerated or overlooked by the person who has been baited because they are counting on the misleading and undesirable tasks eventually paying off. They often assume that these "different and unanticipated" tasks are only temporary and that they will someday transition into the job role and/or assignments they initially were promised.

Sometimes the workplace bait-and-switch happens over time, almost hiding in plain sight. For example, when an organization downsizes its workforce and suddenly the office cubicles look like a ghost town. The remaining staff are often so thankful that their positions were not cut that they are willing to take on more tasks and roles outside of their usual sphere of responsibility. In other words, they end up doing far more work than what they signed up for. This can be tough when they are salaried employees, and their income will not increase alongside the increased workload. This is a definite workplace bait-and-switch, and one that can happen months if not years after obtaining a job.

Helping people avoid getting caught in a bait-and-switch scenario is not easy. Most of the time, a new employee has to start the job and stay in it for a while to recognize whether they have in fact been misled. At first, they might just assume there is some work experience and training that must be acquired before attaining the promised title and or role. Likewise, a longer-tenured employee who sees their workplace change has to ride out long enough to see that things have changed and that those changes are not temporary.

So, what are your options if you have landed in a bait-and-switch situation? While you may be tempted to confront your employer, it is a good idea to think things through before having that conversation. In other words, don't be too hasty or rash. After all, bait-and-switch does not always happen because of an oversight. From what I have seen, it is almost always intentional.

Before having a frank conversation with your employer, I suggest the following steps:

- Carefully review the job posting that you originally applied for. Is there a decent match between the duties that were listed and the ones that you are now being assigned? If there is a good match, it may not be a bait-and-switch scenario. It could just be that there are other things that are bothering you about your new workplace (e.g., boring work, unpleasant colleagues, poor leadership, etc.)
- If promises were made about the type(s) of work that you would be doing once you got oriented and gained some experience, yet the promised work has not yet material-ized, it could be a matter of timing. It is worth having a conversation to determine a timeline during which you can expect to transition into the preferred work that was described to you at the outset. Ideally, you can negotiate a timeline for this transition or ask for more clarity about what other milestones need to be met in order to make the transition.
- Have there been any significant changes at work since you started? If the company's priorities or direction have shifted that may be the reason for the change. Depending on the nature of the change, your employer may not actu-ally have much choice.
- If you cannot find any plausible reasons for the gap between what was promised and what you're experienc-ing, then you'll need to decide whether the actual job is something that you can live with or if you need to start looking for alternative employment options. If you choose to pursue an alternative, the two obvious options are: Negotiating your way into an internal role that is more consistent with what you expected or finding a role in a different organization. If this is where you are, then I do think that you should tread carefully when discussing the issue with your employer. Keep things friendly since you don't want to talk your way into a resignation before you have lined up your next opportunity.

When you find yourself in an unjust bait-and-switch situation, you may feel you have been deceived. You may feel angry. You may be looking for another job. As you do so, try to consider your bait-and-switched job as a runway or launch pad. Think of it as an opportunity to continue to earn income while lining up more suitable employment and/or another source of income. Whatever you do, do it with careful thought, preparation, and when appropriate, some preliminary legal advice in case things go sideways.

TO STAY OR TO GO?

If you were not able to prevent accepting a job in a toxic workplace – or if your job started out alright but then went downhill because of a change in leadership or new people who joined your team, then this next section is for you.

I'm sure you have heard (or thought of) statements like, "At least I'm employed," or "Work isn't supposed to be fun that's why it's called work." And that is a reasonable perspective. No one is saying that going to work every day is comparable to a sunny stroll in the park or your favorite holiday. But it also should not induce depression, paranoia, anxiety, fear, and/or isolation. Sunday nights should not make you lie wide-eyed in bed dreading the approaching week. Unfortunately, most of us have or will experience working in an undesirable organization or as part of a dysfunctional team.

Over the years, I have been approached by employees who have felt uncomfortable in their workplace or have had a long-standing feeling that something is "off" at work. Sometimes they just come to me for a fresh perspective and/or to find an objective sounding board. Other times, they were looking for some support while they figured out whether it was time to move on to a job with a more suitable organizational climate or for help on how to make a graceful exit from an unsustainably difficult workplace. I am grateful for their candor since these interactions have given me access to a rare and intimate perspective. Without breaking confidentiality, I can voice many of the concerns that have been quietly expressed without the individuals involved experiencing any form of retribution or reprisal.

For many people, a job is an integral part of your existence, one that can influence your fulfillment and sense of security. So, what do you do if your job feels like a monotonous trap … or worse, like an abusive relationship? If you come to the realization that your workplace is dreadful, the next question is, should you stay or should you go? Obviously, when you have financial obligations to children, a spouse, a mortgage/rent, student loans, etc., you probably do not want to quit your job before you have something else lined up.

Maybe you are in an administrative government position with benefits and decent hours. Yet each day you sit in a stale cubicle, constantly passed over for promotions you know you deserve because of your skills, experience, and education. Meanwhile, office gossip is being generated around you faster than the assigned work. And once again, you have not been invited for after-work drinks to celebrate a co-worker's birthday. You feel that your boss not only disregards your work but fails to rectify the divisive attitudes in your division or branch. Passive–aggressive workplace bullying and harassment are common, but what is not common is an open dialogue on how to get away from it.

The million-dollar question is, how do I resign without a huge financial loss, or a permanent dent in my resume? A related concern is leaving without a strong reference from your boss. Leaving can also be emotionally challenging, provoking anxiety or even depression, depending on the severity of the mistreatment you have experienced – and the trauma that you're still dealing with. Another concern is finding a new career without relying on your abusive employer as a reference. This can be an intimidating decision, but leaving is critical, just as it is for someone who is in a destructive intimate relationship. To cope and protect yourself, you might try to downplay the severity of the mistreatment you have experienced. The bad actors involved will usually try to diminish the severity too so that they reduce their potential culpability and liability.

It is easier to move from one job to another job than from unemployment to a job. Consequently, I usually advise my clients to try to line up alternative employment before quitting their current job. When it becomes clear that your best or only option is to find another job, the following considerations may help you with your planning:

- It is often easier to think these things through without the financial pressure of unemployment, so invest in some planning while you're still on the payroll.
- Update your resume and LinkedIn profile; sometimes when jobs are posted on LinkedIn you can apply instantly and easily using the "apply using LinkedIn" feature.
- Are there other opportunities in another division or section of the organization (especially if you have a generous pension plan and/or necessary health insurance coverage)?
- Take inventory of your skills and abilities. Where else are they valuable? In which other contexts are your skills, knowledge, and experience relevant?
- Should you consider taking some additional training? Is there anything quick and/or cheap/affordable that may open some doors for you?
- Is there anything that you know a lot about or can offer as a service? This could create consulting or subcontracting opportunities to supplement your income.
- Consider part-time employment elsewhere that helps you develop different skills that you can parlay into something bigger in the long term.
- Consider volunteer experiences, especially in leadership or other responsible roles that may be a good substitute for the lack of a reliable reference from work.
- Take inventory of your accomplishments, successes, and awards over the past 2 to 5 years so that you can highlight them as appropriate in your cover letter, resume, and/or job interviews.
- Consider getting a line of credit and/or building up savings while employed.
- If possible, find at least one ally in the organization who can vouch for you as a reference, perhaps a trusted co-worker or even a client.

- Talk to friends, family or peer contacts who work elsewhere and inquire about leads for other work opportunities.
- If you have only worked under those difficult circumstances for a short period of time and decide to leave, it might be wise to omit the job from your resume, and focus on your cover letter illustrating your education, and work strengths.

NOTES

1 Sull, D., Sull, C., Cipolli, W., & Brighenti, C. (2022, March 16). Why every leader needs to worry about toxic culture. *MIT Sloan Management Review*. https://sloanreview.mit.edu/article/why-every-leader-needs-to-worry-about-toxic-culture/

2 Sull, D., Sull, C., Cipolli, W., & Brighenti, C. (2022, March 16). Why every leader needs to worry about toxic culture. *MIT Sloan Management Review*. https://sloanreview.mit.edu/article/why-every-leader-needs-to-worry-about-toxic-culture/

3 Babiak, P., & Hare, R. D. (2006). *Snakes in suits: When psychopaths go to work*. Regan Books/Harper Collins Publishers. www.harpercollins.com/products/snakes-in-suits-paul-babiakrobert-d-hare?variant=39689396617250

4 Stout, M. (2005). *The sociopath next door: The ruthless versus the rest of us*. New York: Broadway Books. www.penguinrandomhouse.ca/books/174276/the-sociopath-next-door-by-martha-stout-phd/9780767915823/excerpt

5 Reuters in Toronto. (2022, June 15). Toronto police chief apologizes to people of color over disproportionate use of force. *The Guardian*. Retrieved from www.theguardian.com/world/2022/jun/15/toronto-police-people-of-color-face-disproportionate-use-of-force

6 Sull, D., Sull, C., & Zweig, B. (2022, January 11). Toxic culture is driving the great resignation. *MIT Sloan Management Review*. https://sloanreview.mit.edu/article/toxic-culture-is-driving-the-great-resignation/#article-authors

7 Sull, D., Sull, C., Cipolli, W., & Brighenti, C. (2022, March 16). Why every leader needs to worry about toxic culture. *MIT Sloan Management Review*. https://sloanreview.mit.edu/article/why-every-leader-needs-to-worry-about-toxic-culture/

8 Bureau of Labor Statistics, and the Center for American Progress. (2020, July). *The high cost of a toxic workplace culture – how culture impacts the workforce – and the bottom line*. SHRM. https://pmq.shrm.org/wp-content/uploads/2020/07/SHRM-Culture-Report_2019-1.pdf

CHAPTER 7

Identity Is Complex

To say that identity is complex is an extraordinary understatement. Within a social climate where there is a deep, often quiet, and growing backlash against any focus on identity linked to race, gender identity, sexual orientation, religion, or other dimensions often invites criticism of and hostility against the "woke culture." Despite the pushback, no truly inclusive book about facing up to barriers at work is complete without addressing the insidious impact that one's identity can have on one's career. This chapter will include content about the internal processes that are often happening to members of equity-seeking groups. This chapter is meant to support these equity-seeking people who may not have workplace peers or allies to discuss these issues with. The sections within this chapter are also designed to provide insights to anyone who works with and/or wants to be a better ally to members of equity-seeking groups. I will also clarify the concepts of equity, diversity, and inclusion (EDI), systemic racism, discrimination, and related themes.

Many people have heard racialized people say they need to work twice as hard to earn half as much as non-racialized people receive. Among some racialized people, especially Black women, the Superwoman Syndrome is prevalent and toxic. I will address it, since it is common yet often goes unnamed and its implications unexplored.

Periodically, events happen outside of the workplace but capture the attention of most employees. Some of these events, for example, Russia's invasion of Ukraine, garner long-term coverage in the media, both traditional and social, plus ongoing sympathy for the people hurt during these events. Other events take a similar hold on a different

DOI: 10.4324/9781003328988-8

subset of employees. For example, when there are attacks on mosques, synagogues, or churches attended by predominantly Black congregations, when unarmed Black people are killed by police, or there are mass shootings that target Asian, Muslim, Jewish, LBGTQ2+, or Black people. This second category of misfortunate people is often treated differently within the workplace, so in this chapter I'll discuss how values are expressed at work, coded language, and dog whistle expressions. Finally, this chapter wraps up with a discussion of the unique value that racialized leaders can contribute at work and a discussion of how members of underrepresented groups and their allies may position themselves in the future.

COVERING AT WORK

Prior to starting I/O Advisory Services Inc., I was a full-time employee for about 15 years. I enjoyed the earliest parts of my career when I was learning tons and given excellent opportunities to do worthwhile and interesting work. Despite all these positives, when I look back, I realize that there were many downsides associated with being the only Black psychologist (and usually the only Black employee) at work with little diversity to speak of. For the most part, my colleagues were respectful and cooperative, but on some level, I was always an outlier and outsider. To be fair, there were times when I was more extroverted, creative, and entrepreneurial than many of my peers, so that may account for some of my feelings about standing out. It is wonderful and powerful to be unique and valued. But when you are unique and excluded on some level(s), your outsider status can be burdensome.

The way we appear to others influences how they engage with us. Equally important, our identity affects the way we see ourselves and interact with others. In the workplace, this dynamic has immense implications – especially because (historically) certain identities were preferred and welcomed while others were tolerated or even excluded. The residual effects from this legacy still plague workplaces today.

Years after starting I/O Advisory Services Inc., I came across the concept of "Covering at Work." A 2019 report published by Deloitte titled "Uncovering talent – a new model of inclusion"[1] claimed that the majority of certain populations in the workplace actively cover up aspects of their identities that they believe are unwelcome and/or stigmatized. In other words, they are intentionally downplaying who they are. Deloitte's report revisited work done by Erving Goffman in his 1963 book *Stigma: Notes on the Management of Spoiled Identity.*[2] For example, the 2019 Deloitte study found that women, members of pride communities, and racialized people are covering at work. The study also showed that, to some extent, almost 50% of white men were also covering. The white men were downplaying or concealing a disability, a political affiliation that was different from the majority of their peers, or that they were in an intimate relationship with a racialized person.

Overall, Deloitte 2019 reported that 61% of the 3,129 respondents reported covering along at least one of four dimensions – appearance, affiliation (i.e., avoiding behaviors associated with their identity to offset negative stereotypes about that identity, whereby moms may avoid discussing their children to avoid the perception that she's less committed to her work), advocacy (i.e, sticking up for or defending their group), or association (i.e., avoiding contact with other group members, for example, if a lesbian woman avoids bringing her wife to a work-related event). Specifically, 83% of LGBTQ2+ individuals, 79% of Black people, 67% of women of color, 66% of non-racialized women, 63% of Hispanics, and 45% of straight men reported covering. Each of these respondents worked for organizations that had implemented inclusion policies and/or practices related to race and ethnicity.

WORKPLACE TRAUMA AND COVERING

Although not addressed in Deloitte's work, in my opinion, covering at work is a *response* to racial and other forms of trauma that are caused by any form of discrimination and/ or exclusion (e.g., anti-Black racism, other forms of racism, homophobia, disability status, transphobia, Islamophobia, xenophobia, etc.).

For BIPOC/BAME employees particularly, racial trauma shows up after exposure to racism and can produce mental and physical effects and consequences. In response to this trauma, the fight or flight instincts are triggered, and physical symptoms can develop including an increase in the stress hormone cortisol which triggers a higher heart rate, weight gain, slowed physical healing, muscle weakness, increased symptoms related to anxiety, depression, and hypervigilance. Racial trauma can also happen after seeing something that you may not have experienced directly. One example is witnessing colleagues' or peers' experiences of racism, seeing racism play out on traditional and social media, etc. It also includes the trauma experienced indirectly through stories heard from family members (intergenerational racial trauma). Scientific research[3] now suggests that racial trauma can be passed on to successive generations through epigenetics. Other forms of discrimination, based on religion, sexual orientation, sexual identity, disability, etc. follow the same general pattern – even if the person's identity as a member of an equity-seeking group is invisible.

IMPLICATIONS OF COVERING

I would argue that frequent or periodic experiences of microaggressions and/or more blatant forms of discrimination are so common in some workplaces that the self-protection that manifests as covering may be subconscious and automatic. In his 2021 book *What Happened to You? Conversations on Trauma, Resilience, and Healing*[4] (co-written with Oprah Winfrey) neuroscientist and psychiatrist, Dr. Bruce Perry explains that, when someone experiences enough of these "small t" traumas caused by discrimination, exclusion, microaggressions, etc., the impact can be on par with typical "big T" traumas associated with serious car accidents, assaults, etc. The difference is that people who have survived major or "big T" traumas are often treated differently. They are provided with support to help them recover. This rarely happens to people who have been burdened with a lifetime of experience with systemic and/or individual racism or other forms of discrimination. Given that a person's livelihood is also tied into this dynamic, it is no surprise that to prevent or minimize further pain caused by exclusion, denial of promotions, and other advantages, covering at work takes hold.

This means that a lot of mental and creative energy is being diverted into covering – or protecting oneself – instead of doing one's actual work because of real or perceived workplace expectations. It is also likely that, despite having diversity within a workforce, the organization is not reaping the rewards because its "diverse" talents are isolated rather than fully embraced and integrated into teams and informal relationships. As a wise VP noted after I explained this concept to her, theoretically, many organizations are paying for a 100% effort, but they are only benefiting from a lower effort because their employees are spending some percentage of their mental and emotional energy on self-protection from a hostile work environment.

There is another consequence of covering at work worth noting. When you are intentionally or unintentionally hiding something as you interact with others at work and create professional relationships, the quality of those relationships tends to suffer. When we are guarded and in self-protection mode rather than straightforward and authentic, we may come across as aloof, hard to know, or in some cases, insincere. So, in other words, covering hurts our "knowability" and becomes a barrier to establishing the types of trusting relationships that are important for professional networking. If someone does not feel that they know you or trust you, it is hard for them to advocate for you by telling others about you or vouching for you when opportunities arise.

The prevalence of covering at work implies that most people (i.e., 61% of the people who reported covering on at least one dimension) may not be developing the best products and services that they are capable of because of their preoccupations with self-protection. This hurts the individual's work output and the organization's bottom line. On an individual and personal level, I would argue that this ultimately comes down to employees' psychological safety. When someone feels psychologically safe rather than threatened or unsafe, they don't need to cover. Ideally, and in principle, ensuring this basic human right for all employees should be a given. Otherwise stated, inclusion is a moral imperative and also a practical imperative for organizations.

In addition to covering at work taking a toll on an employee's productivity and creativity, it's easy to see how it may also take a toll on their mental health. Although it is common to act in a more reserved and professional way at work, when the gap between your *personal self* and your *professional/public self* is wide, it can be draining. Feeling like you must routinely put on an act can be tiring and difficult to sustain over the long term. This intentional role-playing seems different than simply maintaining appropriate professional boundaries while at work. For example, choosing to not read or reply to work-related emails after 7 pm on workdays and not dating one's colleagues (i.e., maintaining professional boundaries) feels qualitatively different from covering up one's sexual orientation or status as an immigrant or racialized person.

For most of the time that I was an employee, I was also the mother of a young child … and for a while I was navigating a time-consuming and draining separation and divorce while working and parenting. With so much going on, I doubt that covering at work was ever conscious. It was more of an automatic survival technique, much like code switching (i.e., switching among dialects, styles, or vernaculars depending on who you're interacting with) to make professional inter-actions easier for the person or people with whom I was interacting.

Covering at work was not because of a lack of confidence or shame. Rather, it was because in some respects, I knew that my behavioral style and perspective as a Black woman was not necessarily understood or preferred. At a risk of seeming arrogant, I will acknowledge that I was bright, a fast learner, articulate, perceptive, funny, hard-working, creative, and

I got along with others. Those are all admirable qualities. But I am also a Black, Canadian-born woman of Jamaican and Ghanaian descent. These are also admirable qualities and identities, but in the context of a work environment that implicitly prioritized, centered, and valued a very specific type of person and viewpoint, anything different was treated as though it was less valuable and secondary. To paraphrase from Deloitte's 2019[5] inclusion report, when employees look at the leaders within an organization, and see that most, if not all, are the same gender, age, ethnic/racial background, and seem to share similar values, they pick up the message that to be successful in that organization, you need to fit in with the existing norms. Acquiring training and gaining relevant experience to improve the odds of advancement is reasonable. But, when advancement seems to require that you have a different, age, gender, racial/ethnic background, and other superficial characteristics, it's no wonder why certain people realize they are not a good fit and leave for another organization.

When there's nothing that you can do to fit that narrow, idealized prototype, it is tempting for employees to start looking for other opportunities. This is also part of why representation matters so much. If you want to create and retain a diverse workforce, it is essential that the organizational climate is inclusive enough that people do not feel compelled to cover at work in order to have worth. It is exhausting, and given the chance, your best talent (who feel compelled to cover something that has little to do with their talent) will leave to find a workplace that is more comfortable because it is inclusive. When a client has the option to accept an opportunity in organizations where there is a better and more inclusive culture, I usually support their decisions to go where they are wanted and accepted.

Although covering at work is a mostly internal process that may not be noticeable to others, it can hurt your work performance because when you are preoccupied by self-protection you have less energy to put towards your work, creativity, and innovation. And when you feel obligated to cover at work, you are much less likely to be authentic and want to engage with your colleagues and superiors in ways that enhance those relationships. Without much of a connection to your coworkers and bosses it means that you are out of the loop, making it much easier to be overlooked and passed over for promotions. Furthermore, the figurative armor that you may wear when protecting yourself from potential emotional harm makes it harder for others to get to know you. Many may see you as guarded or aloof, which makes it harder for others to feel that they know you well enough to vouch for you or make introductions that can lead to advancement.

DIVERSITY, EQUITY, AND INCLUSION

As social justice issues have risen to the forefront of public discourse, a residual effect has been employers adopting buzzwords like *diversity*, *equity*, and *inclusion* as aspirational qualities of their workplace environment. While the use of these words has become more prevalent, it is important that they are defined appropriately. That way, a workplace environment that claims to be diverse and inclusive can be measured against the actual meaning of the words. As explained by Jennifer Brown (2016) in *Inclusion: Diversity, The New Workplace & The Will to Change*[6] – diversity is *the who and the what*: Who is being hired, who is sitting around the table and involved in the decisions, who is being mentored and promoted? In contrast, inclusion is *the how*. Inclusion is *the behaviors that welcome and embrace diversity*. If you are an inclusive leader, you know how to support and integrate a full diversity of perspectives and identities.

In contrast, equity is an approach that ensures that everyone has access to the same opportunities. Equity acknowledges that barriers and advantages exist, and that as a result, everyone does not start from the same place. Equity is a process that recognizes unequal starting points and makes a commitment to correct and address the imbalance or built-in unfairness.

There has been a long-standing perception that in Canada there really isn't much racism. This sentiment is due in part to the existence of the Charter of Rights and Freedoms which states that:

> Every individual is equal before and under the law and has the right to the equal protection and equal benefit of the law without discrimination and, in particular, without discrimination based on race, national or ethnic origin, color, religion, sex, age or mental or physical disability.
>
> (Canadian Charter of Rights and Freedoms Section 15(1)[7])

In addition, officially, Canada has a policy of multiculturalism, so it is easy to assume that diversity, equity, and inclusion are automatically built-in. The fact is, however, that Canada's history includes clear examples of individual and systemic racism directed at Indigenous and Black people. From 1671 to 1831, Indigenous people and Black people were enslaved – and this occurred before Canada's official status as a country in 1867. Since that time, there have been countless milestones, including Indian residential schools, denial of land grants to Blacks, expropriation of land and homes owned by Indigenous and Black people, the presence of the Klu Klux Klan, Japanese internment camps, and the Chinese head tax. American history is more well known because of its widespread and longer-lasting chattel slavery where African people were captured, dehumanized, and exploited for financial gain for approximately 400 years. Even without elaborating on these examples, these events and behaviors are not consistent with modern multiculturalism, diversity, equity, or inclusion. The legacy of this troubling past has not been erased by an official policy of multiculturalism and non-discrimination. Countless Canadians and Americans grew up without learning this history. At the same time, they were taught, directly or indirectly, that racialized people are less successful because they are inferior or lack a good work ethic.

In the time that has passed since the original work by Deloitte was first published, a more recent study of 700 Canadian men and women identifying as Black, East Asian, and South Asian by the non-profit women's advocacy organization

Catalyst in partnership with Ascend Canada found that Canadian people of color carry an extra weight at work that's so significant and burdensome that it impacts their health and often causes them to contemplate quitting. The weight is known as an "emotional tax" – a palpable feeling of being different from peers at work because of one's gender, race, or ethnicity, which can affect a person's well-being and ability to thrive in their job (Tara Deschamps,[8] July 19, 2019).

Armed with even a basic awareness of the struggles that certain people have been dealing with, there is a chance that fair-minded non-racialized people will understand the legitimate need for diversity, equity, and inclusion. So, whether you are a co-worker, leader, or business owner, the workplace culture that you contribute to may have a bigger impact than you know. Your stated versus practiced values communicate what is accepted at work and may be tied to career outcomes, psychological safety, and productivity.

SYSTEMIC RACISM, DISCRIMINATION, AND RELATED TRAINING

Systemic or institutional racism includes the ways that the white experience is used as the default or standard, whilst racialized people are treated as secondary and less important – and how this is reflected and upheld in a society's systems or institutions. The unstated subtext is that white people are superior to racialized people. This is manifest in seemingly neutral policies, rules, and laws that have a differential impact that benefits some individuals (usually white) and simultaneously hurts others (usually BIPOC/BAME). Systemic racism does not require that individuals have bad intent or active awareness.

Systemic racism is sometimes brushed upon in the context of largely superficial diversity and inclusion initiatives that acknowledge unconscious bias but offer little in terms of concrete steps designed to offset the real problems. Ironically and unfortunately, many of the best-paid consultants who use diversity and inclusion in their branding and promotional materials profit off the negative experiences of the very people they should be advocating for. This means that in many organizations, race and other forms of identity are not addressed in a meaningful or impactful way. This also means that work becomes an alienating and lonely place for countless employees. Equally bad, people have been judged by their identity as a racialized or Indigenous person, member of an LBGTQ2+ community, religious minority, disabled person, etc. instead of being judged for what they can contribute at work.

Although systemic racism has historically (and quietly) been part of most workplaces, suddenly it became a hot and public topic during the summer of 2020. Events that occurred that summer compounded with prior incidents in Canada, the United States, and elsewhere highlighted a global culture of racism. In my experience, people who are most affected by systemic racism might discuss it with their close friends and family, but rarely will they do so openly with coworkers who are not also negatively affected by it. Typically, racialized employees find that their coworkers choose to ignore or avoid weighing in on social or political issues that do not affect them personally – a choice that's linked to earned or unearned privilege. Earned privileges include things like formal education or titles (e.g., Dr., Reverend, or Justice). Unearned privileges include white skin, heterosexuality, and being able-bodied. Having privilege does not mean you do not have to work hard or that you don't experience struggle, rather it simply means that you have certain advantages. Some people have the privilege of being able to avoid dealing with social and political issues because these issues do not create potential harm for them. Further, since those issues are not personal, and they do not see themselves as allies or advocates, they can simply disregard them. At its core, ignoring injustice and unfairness and tolerating incivility is part of how words and values escalate into negative impact. When people deny the humanity of others, for example, by diminishing the impact of unsupportive or mean-spirited behavior, it is easier to overlook or even rationalize others' mistreatment. This dehumanization is part of how words and thoughts manifest into actions like harassment and bullying and create work environments that are not inclusive.

The workplace continues to collide with many socially and politically charged movements, and acts of protest against racist practices. Consider the widely publicized circumstances of former National Football League (NFL) player Colin Kaepernick who was black-balled and disparaged for kneeling in protest of police brutality before some of his games. Or in Canada when two federal elected officials took to Twitter to debate the merits of considering versus ignoring the different experiences and obstacles faced by people of color, people with disabilities, immigrants, LGBTQ2+, etc. When the *Huffington Post* published a summary of the ongoing feud, the Black elected politician Celina Caesar Chavannes faced a strong and hostile backlash for calling out racism. The anger and opposition that she was obligated to handle – as a Black woman with influence – sent a sad and discouraging message to other victims of racism who were considering speaking out. Whether on the football field or in the halls of government, the racist experience of the employee who spoke out – in whatever form it may have been – was met with contempt, intolerance, and insensitivity.

High-profile incidents such as those described above certainly create a buzz. But consider the countless smaller, more private spaces and interactions in which a BIPOC/BAME person or someone with another minority status navigates daily minefields at work – and outside of work. Bias and discriminatory behavior may show up as whispers in the hallway or the boardroom – actions that are less explicit and less sensational but nonetheless still leave the person feeling marginalized due to their race.

Years ago, I remember a visceral and public example of racial bias when two Black men were arrested at a Starbucks in the United States, for "having the audacity" to wait at a table for an associate to arrive before purchasing their beverages. Upon hearing their explanation, the Starbucks employee demanded the men leave and then called the police, an act widely considered unreasonable and racist.

I had always thought of Starbucks as a progressive employer, since their employees demonstrate all types of diversity (e.g., age, gender identity, race, religion, etc.), so I was not surprised when they acted swiftly. They made a public apology and fired the person who had called the police. Starbucks also announced it would close more than 8,000 of its shops in the United States to offer racial bias training. Similar training took place in Canada in June 2018. These actions showed some goodwill even if they will not solve the problem completely.

This training came on the heels of other random and downright bizarre incidents that had been covered in the news in Canada and the United States. At Yale University, police were called because a Black student was asleep in a common room ... in her dorm. In Oakland, CA, someone called the police because Black people were having a BBQ in a park where picnics and barbequing were common and expected.

During the times of these incidents, I was a self-employed consultant and coach rather than a typical employee with colleagues. I thought about the water cooler conversations that must have been happening in workplaces, universities, NFL franchise locations, government offices, and Starbucks shops. Blatant racism was happening – and it was being reported by the traditional media and via social media. The leadership in these organizations was probably feeling the heat. The employees in so many organizations were probably left wondering, *well ... what about me?* Will these training sessions and other related interventions ever become concrete enough to make a difference in my workplace? Enhance my career mobility? Improve my livelihood? When there are no obvious or encouraging answers for an employee, considering more progressive employers that may offer a better and more inclusive workplace culture and fit becomes entirely appropriate – and likely.

So, here is the question: Even if well-intended, does one day of sensitivity or anti-bias training change the racial discrimination that exists in organizations? The short answer is usually no. It may even fuel a resentful backlash ... because this is much more complex than just retraining/ educating workers about their "diverse customer base." It should include reflection on earned and unearned privilege and a discussion of the profound harm and implications of discrimination.

Sensitivity and anti-bias training don't begin to address the experiences or needs of employees who are not white and have been dealing with systemic discrimination and the unfair limits placed on their career mobility. One day or a series of training sessions should be part of a larger culture change and an adjustment to hiring and promotion policies and practices.

Through experience, I know that a quick, sanitized mes-sage encouraging employees to "get along and don't say anything that isn't politically correct (PC)" does not work. When an organization's stated versus practiced values do not match, the inconsistency can create even more tension. When the central issues are not being taken seriously, many people understand the intentional use of coded language and dog whistle expressions. To them, the problem is not about people needing more sensitivity, but rather not being racist (or sexist, or ableist, or homophobic, or transphobic, or Islamophobic, xenophobic, etc.) ... at work. More recently, organizations have been hiring leaders and specialists who can bring anti-racist perspectives and practices into their organizations. Often, these chief diversity officers and their teams can re-work policies and procedures through an anti-racism anti-oppression lens to make sure that their impact is equivalent to all employees, regardless of their identity. There is often room to tighten up loopholes where biases slip in under the guise of discretion in the decision-making process. The impact of these diversity and inclusion and/or anti-racism units/directorates is often mixed and depends on who these leaders report to and the resources that they have to work with. This satirical yet painfully accurate article "How to Lose a Chief Diversity Officer in 6 Months"[9] spells out some of the main reasons why people in these roles are sometimes set up for failure.

THE SUPERWOMAN SYNDROME

In some workplaces, I have noticed the troubling perception that to achieve a diverse workforce the standards need to be lowered. In my opinion, this sentiment is empty and misleading and does not hold up under scrutiny. Instead, what I have noticed is that when a racialized person is hired or promoted, they are often better qualified, harder working, and more experienced than their non-BIPOC counterparts. Why? They had to be, or they would never have gotten a foot in the door in the first place. When you also consider that they are performing at a high level while also using some percentage of their mental and emotional energy to self-protect, or cover at work, this is even more impressive. In some respects, it seems like a superpower.

One year, I was asked to speak at an International Women's Day event that was being organized by Sigma Beta Phi Sorority in Ottawa, one of the few Black sororities in Canada. I was intrigued since, aside from attending some step competitions featuring Black fraternities and sororities in the United States, I had not been close to "Greek life." Plus, their topic, the "Superwoman Syndrome," added another level of fascination.

I had an idea in my head about what the superwoman syndrome was, but I was curious to know if my perception matched reality. Here's the definition that Sigma Beta Phi provided:

> The superwoman syndrome is the perception that one must be perfect in all things: perfect on the job, at home, in one's body image, in one's relationships, etc. and it is exacerbated by other social pressures.

The sorority asked me to address how I have combatted the superwoman syndrome and/or any implications for mental health, particularly among women of color or members of other underrepresented groups (e.g., women with disabilities, Indigenous women, women in the LGBTQ2+ community, etc.). In addition, they said it would be helpful if I could also provide insight into how external influences can either help or hinder the mental health of these types of women.

For as long as I can remember, I have been preoccupied with the demands of my personal and professional life. Though I had not really thought about it in the context of the superwoman syndrome, there is no doubt that I have felt its pressure over the years. And for the sorority to prioritize the topic meant that they believe many other Black women identify with those pressures as well. I would argue that in addition to getting closer to the top of my game professionally, as a Black woman, there have been a few extra layers of difficulty.

Layer #1: The Superwoman Syndrome
While Covering at Work

To be a superwoman is a difficult thing. But to be a superwoman while shielding aspects of your identity is an exhausting ordeal. The superwoman is probably using a great deal of mental and creative energy to cover at work in addition to doing her actual work. The real or perceived workplace expectations on top of the burden of perfection in other areas of life when mixed with anxiety and burnout is a challenging blend.

Layer #2: The Superwoman Syndrome
While Being the One and Only

In January 2019, Sneader and Yee, with McKinsey & Company published the results of their study "One Is the Loneliest Number."[10] They asked 64,000 employees from 279 companies in North America. The authors pointed out that often when we're the *only one* ... a woman in an all-male environment, the only person of color, the only LGBTQ2+ person, or whatever, these experiences created anxiety, pressure, and the feeling of being on the spot, that if we did or said the wrong thing, negative stereotypes would get reinforced, or biases confirmed. That ongoing scrutiny, unhelpful stereotyping, and sustained pressure can be extremely draining.

When you are the "only," there is a good chance that there is nobody at work who you can discuss your circumstances with. To provide a bit of a reality check, I'll share some red flags or indicators that workplace culture is not as inclusive as it could or should be. That way, it will be another set of criteria that you can use to reinforce or develop more clarity about your workplace culture – and any potential implications for your peace of mind and wellness.

Red Flags about Workplace Culture for "Onlys"

- BAME/BIPOC and members of other equity-seeking groups get hired but they do not stay.
- BAME/BIPOC employees do not participate in non-mandatory social events or team-building exercises.
- BAME/BIPOC employees and other minorities are well-represented at the lower levels, but they are largely absent from leadership.

In fairness, this representation issue might also be linked to pipelines of potential employees. For instance, in the field of Psychology so few racialized students are admitted to graduate programs in Canada that it makes it quite hard to have diversity among professionals in college or university faculty, or in industry/the profession writ large. The situation is somewhat better in the United States but there is still underrepresentation.

Layer #3: The Superwoman Syndrome
While Compensating for Prejudice

Through the magic of LinkedIn, I "met" Tanya Janca, a woman who is a superstar in tech. In a January 2019 article published on Medium (which has since been deleted), she argued that "something that is little talked about in the tech industry is the concept of 'Compensating for Prejudice'; actions that we have to take to offset negative perceptions due to being a member of the minority within our industry."

Janca is a white woman working in a male-dominated field. She understands what it is like to be an only. To some extent, her insights match my experiences of being the only Black psychologist (and usually the only racialized person) in just about every employment or business environment that I've been in since my graduate school training in the late 1990s. The misogyny, being underestimated, and overlooked or ignored described by Janca are familiar. As a white woman, however, Janca is not likely to endure exclusion by white identifying people or life-threatening risks because of the color of her skin in the way that a Black person will. Although, I have not dwelled on it in the past (mostly because of the demands of single parenting, post-divorce, while working full-time), there is something very wrong with these demographics, since Black psychologists are still so rare in Canada and the United States.

Here are some of Janca's concrete examples of how she has compensated for being part of a small minority. She reported proving herself, before being asked to prove herself because she had been challenged, over and over, throughout her entire career. She also recalled dropping mentions of the amount of time she had already spent working in her field and highlighting her accomplishments.

In addition to compensating for the gender-based discrimination that she experienced, Janca noted that she was not invited to key meetings, was not assigned to important projects, and did not receive the same opportunities, promotions, or pay. She was being excluded, overlooked, and underestimated, time and time again. Again, all of these experiences capture some of the experiences of BAME/BIOPC employees in predominantly white organizations and that members of other equity-seeking groups experience. Although her descriptions are accurate, I would argue that being a white woman in Science, Technology, Engineering, and Mathematics (STEM) is different than being Black in a predominantly white environment. Anti-Black racism carries far harsher and intersectional consequences. White women are not denied as many work-related opportunities or killed exclusively because of the color of their skin. Clearly, dealing with all of this while also being a superwoman is even tougher than it looks.

On a personal note, I have experienced versions of all of the above. As a grad student, I was always the "only" and "compensating for prejudice" in every single course. During my professional life in the government, again I was always the "only" and sometimes "compensating for prejudice" and to some extent, "covering at work" by downplaying how differently I saw and experienced many situations and circumstances. I won't say that any of this was necessarily intentional since I am certain that many of my colleagues were and are well-intentioned. They were also preoccupied with the realities of making a living, raising their families, etc. There is no doubt, however, that many of these consequences were systemic and structural. Since starting my practice in 2012, most of my experiences and interactions in the business community have been as the "only" Black person at an event or meeting. Although there have been allies along the way who were supportive and respectful of what I represented and had to offer, there have also been times when I have had to prove myself, explain my professional background, and take other actions designed to help me claim my space. There are so many ways that some people compensate for others' negative and unfounded prejudices.

It may be shocking, but pre-pandemic and before the gruesome and visceral murder of George Floyd, this low-key racism had become so common and normalized that it was only when someone was experiencing something similar and/or wished to discuss it with me that I reflected and remembered. Otherwise, I barely considered it. This was all just part of the difficult but common reality of being a Black professional in a predominantly white environment. During the Covid-19 pandemic, however, I noticed a shift. Suddenly, popular people who had become influential despite a lack of special skills or knowledge started to take a back seat to various experts. For example, pre-pandemic, Jenny McCarthy's (American actress and model) commentary about a perceived link between vaccines and autism were higher profile than evidence-based information from medical specialists, researchers, and health-focused organization like the Centers for Disease Control and Prevention in the United States or the World Health Organization (WHO). From the start of the Covid-19 pandemic, less "polished" people with relevant and specialized knowledge started to dominate the traditional and social media (e.g., Dr. Anthony S. Fauci, physician–scientist and immunologist serving as the director of the National Institute of Allergy and Infectious Diseases and the Chief Medical Advisor to President Joe Biden and Dr. Tedros Ghebreyesus,

Director-General, WHO). For months, the local airwaves and the Internet were dominated by ordinary-looking people who normally would never be featured despite their expertise. These humble people with big degrees and complicated foreign-sounding names became important. To some extent, I rode that wave. People sought me out because I was knowledgeable because of my professional background and my unique lived experiences.

I must admit that perhaps as a function of maturity, or for professional branding, I don't try to blend in. Instead, I revel in the fact that I am different from 99% of all other industrial and organizational psychologists, executive coaches, career coaches, and HR consultants. That is often the precise reason why people seek me out. This is why I have also encouraged many of my clients to identify what makes them unique, embrace these differences, and try to stand out by being known for their excellence. It is hard to identify anyone, notorious or not, who has ever accomplished anything significant in life, and who completely blended in with everyone else.

HOW VALUES ARE EXPRESSED AT WORK

Starting around 2015, I noticed that the subtext of many stories covered by the mainstream media in Canada and the United States included increasingly overtly racist and xenophobic perspectives. In Canada, there were federal politicians who were vying to become the next Prime Minister who were saying things that were blatantly anti-Muslim and anti-immigrant. For example, one candidate for re-election made a campaign promise to create a "snitch line" where people could report neighbors and others who they deemed were engaging in "barbaric cultural practices"[11] to the national police force, the Royal Canadian Mounted Police (RCMP). This federal candidate also promised to increase funding to help international organizations fight against child marriages. At the time, there were already laws on the books that made it illegal to engage in human trafficking and child marriage. The political party associated with the proposed

(Canadian) Zero Tolerance for Barbaric Cultural Practices Act also wanted to ensure that Muslim women could not wear their niqab during Canadian citizenship ceremonies. In my opinion, the goal was to appeal to anti-Muslim sentiments without saying the word Muslim. Similarly, there was a calculated intention to make it seem as though Muslim people frequently engaged in inappropriate cultural practices, when in reality, there were probably as many right-wing Christian terrorist extremists, domestic terrorists, and white supremacists as there were Muslim extremists, yet there was no "snitch" line to hold members of those groups accountable, nor was anyone proposing one.

The same pattern was clear in the 2016 U.S. presidential election where Hilary Clinton and Donald Trump were rivals. Although this trend has nothing to do with the typical workplace, it has had an impact. To be fair, from 2015 to 2020, I was not part of a traditional workplace – I was an external consultant and coach. For that I was extremely grateful. During that time, I knew that if I had been an employee, I would wonder where I stood when my colleagues and/or employer remained silent – especially when things literally started burning by the summer of 2020 following the murder of George Floyd, an unarmed Black man, who was choked to death by police officer Derek Chauvin who pinned Floyd's neck to the ground with his knee. This gruesome murder was watched by several onlookers with camera phones who implored the police to stop. Even worse, three of Chauvin's co-workers helped to pin Floyd to the ground. I know that I am not alone in this regard. I personally know Muslim and Jewish people who have experienced similar feelings when major events have terrorized and/or killed members of their communities. Similarly, quite a few Black employees told me that they felt isolated, unsupported, and uncomfortable during the summer of 2020 when their employers and colleagues said nothing despite the worldwide social justice protests against systemic discrimination and anti-Black racism.

This pattern repeated itself in many U.S. and Canadian workplaces in May 2022 when an 18-year-old white supremacist man killed ten Black people at a Buffalo, New York grocery store. He live-streamed his premeditated mass murder via social media, so viewers saw his gun with the N-word painted on the barrel. These same viewers saw the gunman apologize to white shoppers and then continue to kill Black ones. Also evident was the callous and graphic way that he sometimes doubled back to shoot fallen victims again to ensure their demise. After two years of equity, diversity, and inclusion training and commitments to do better, many Black employees and their allies were struck by the hypocrisy of the silence within their workplaces – especially after a prolonged show of support for Ukrainian people from a different continent.

For years, many people have quietly been living in a state of provoked anxiety and sadness due to what's happening to people who look like them in the broader society and around the world. Sometimes it has been due to events such as the fallout from the niqab debate during the 2015 Canadian federal election in Canada. It has also involved hate crimes leading up to and following Brexit in the United Kingdom and surrounding the U.S. Presidential Election in 2016 and its aftermath. For example, the White Nationalists' demonstration in Charlottesville, VA during the summer of 2017 or other hate crimes where people were injured or killed. In all cases, the targeted people, Muslims, immigrants, Blacks, Mexicans, Jews, and members of the LGBTQ2+ community, have been made to feel inferior and unwelcome. The well-publicized murders of George Floyd, Breonna Taylor, Ahmaud Arbery, and too many others in 2020 accelerated and amplified the Black Lives Matter movement and greater awareness of related social justice concerns. We saw a similar pattern with members of various Asian communities singled out for insults, attacks, and even murder (e.g., the shootings in Atlanta, Georgia in March 2021 and countless other incidents in the United States and in Canada, especially in British Columbia). Many of these issues have been awkward to discuss because they have been linked to politics or politicians… and we have been conditioned to avoid talking about those subjects. The assumption is that it is impolite (and unwise) to talk about politics or religion.

OK, fine, most of us can agree that politics (and religion) have no place in polite conversation – especially at work. But what about values? As employers, leaders, and colleagues who are allies, can we explore our values at work? Are we allowed to talk about tolerance? Racism? How about inclusion? Double standards? Harassment? ... Even fear?

I want to make a distinction between the various types of values that might be at play. First there are *implicit values,* which are usually unwritten, may be unconscious, but they guide what is happening in an organization or a broader society. For instance, the founder of an organization may value humor and, although this is unstated, it shows up in the tone on the organization's website and the lighthearted atmosphere among colleagues. Next, there are *stated values.* These are public and they may be written explicitly on the organization's website and found in onboarding documents (e.g., Code of Conduct, zero-tolerance on harassment and bullying, diversity, and inclusion statements, etc.). Finally, there are *practiced values.* Practiced values reflect what is happening in an organization. For example, an organization can state that there is no tolerance for harassment and bullying but when it happens, in practice, the aggressors are not held accountable for their bad behavior. When these values do not match, the people who are paying attention will focus on the practiced values and govern themselves accordingly. This is true in professional one-on-one relationships, within teams, and from an organizational perspective.

CODED LANGUAGE AND DOG WHISTLE EXPRESSIONS

Biases and systemic discrimination are not limited to the workplace. These problems also exist in the business community where many self-employed people earn their livelihoods, so we'll focus on that sector.

Some years after starting my firm, I was invited to be featured in a video about the benefits of doing business in the city where I live and work – and the advantages of joining a local business association. Although I appreciated the opportunity, I had received a set of talking points that made me feel uncomfortable and insulted. I was conflicted. I was still growing my business, so I wanted the advantages associated with the potential additional exposure. At the same time, I had no intention of selling my soul or disrespecting much of what I hold dear. As a mature and practical person, I also did not want to embarrass my local Chamber of Commerce since I still needed/wanted their cooperation.

I recognized a lot of coded language and dog whistle expressions in the invitation disguised as proposed themes, questions, and speaking points. As a work and business psychologist and a woman of color, I know plenty about both. Coded language is when people use words that on the surface seem neutral, but they are consciously or subconsciously intended to mean something else. For example, the line and political campaign slogan, "Make America Great Again" can be taken at face value, or it can be interpreted as "Make America like it used to be … when women, LGBTQ2+, immigrants, non-Christians, and people of color knew their place … and knew when to shut up." That one statement excludes and marginalizes a vast group of people who believe that the America of the past was far from ideal. For some of these people, the slogan literally hits like a punch to the gut.

Similarly, "dog whistle" expressions or comments are those that seem impartial on the surface but mean something very different to people who share a particular attitude or ideology. Just as only dogs can hear a high-pitched dog whistle, only people who are attuned to a particular style of thinking and interpretation "hear" these "dog whistle" expressions. For instance, when a Canadian candidate for political office suggests creating the aforementioned "snitch line" for reporting "barbaric cultural practices" even though the national police force – the Royal Canadian Mounted Police (RCMP) – and other police organizations already have mechanisms in place for reporting illegal behavior, it can be taken at least two ways. One interpretation is that it is innocent and only about keeping residents safe. Another interpretation is that this is a good way to report on immigrants and Muslims when you do not like their perceived values or behavior. This is a polite way of ensuring a sense of unwelcome to certain groups of people, without having to use obvious offensive language or ideology.

After I had agreed to be in a video about the benefits of doing business in my city and the advantages of joining a local business association, I was perplexed by the questions directed specifically at me. With two advanced degrees, and as a successful business owner who lives in a respectable upper middle-class neighborhood, I didn't like the subtext associated with why I was expected to paraphrase from a script focusing on inexpensive real estate, discounts available to members of the business organization, and a culture of diversity, openness, and generosity in the community.

On the surface, these are all reasonable and neutral concepts to explore. But when the *only* person asked to address these issues is the racialized person and all the other (white members) in the video focus exclusively on their businesses, the benefits of networking, operating their business in their city along with advantages of joining a local business association, it reinforces harmful stereotypes, inequalities, and systemic racism. I also share this story to show that having a title like "Dr.," living in a good neighborhood, and being successful does not fully insulate Black people from racism.

To break it down further, if I had been the only one of 6 to 8 people who talks about inexpensive real estate, then I would have reinforced the stereotype that people of color can't afford more expensive/better quality housing. I should mention that some of the other business owners to be featured in the videos lived in my neighborhood! If I, the only racialized person in the video, am the only one who talks about discounts associated with their membership in the business association, then I am reinforcing a subtext where racialized people need discounts, but others don't. When members of the majority group do not talk about culture, diversity, or openness but the racialized person does, it assigns the responsibility to those who are already marginalized to discuss their marginalization by the majority group. In addition, it uses the racialized person as a prop who's been pigeonholed to promote a sense of inclusion while majority group members simultaneously exclude minorities from other business and success-related themes.

Using the general parameters that I was originally given, I rewrote the business association's script. I addressed the original themes in a way that was still accurate but did not reinforce unhelpful stereotypes that may offend racialized people or hurt my reputation or professional brand. Equally important, my revised script highlighted my contributions and accomplishments as a successful business owner. In other words, I edited out the coded language and dog whistle expressions, and my revisions were tactful and did not publicly shame or alienate the folks who had invited me to be featured in the video. Of course, all of this required hidden and unpaid labor that my white business associates did not have to contribute.

There is a chance that no harm was intended when the association wrote the script for me, and the fact that my modifications were accepted was encouraging. As angry and disappointed as I was, I could have called out that organization with some not-so-coded language of my own. As a single parent who was self-employed in a predominantly white environment, I definitely needed to choose my battles without violating my principles. Instead, I decided to lead with maturity and wisdom by not engaging with the questions and answers that I didn't feel were appropriate to my cause.

THE UNIQUE VALUE OF RACIALIZED LEADERS

One aspect of diversity that is often overlooked and/or misunderstood is the unique contributions and impact that racialized leaders can make. When it comes to understanding the financial implications of decisions, the banking industry and stock exchanges are exemplars. So, I took notice when the "smart money" in banking and the Nasdaq stock exchange poised themselves to avoid making expensive mistakes by taking a different approach to corporate leadership.

In December 2020, global law firm Cooley LLP[12] reported that Nasdaq, a global electronic marketplace for buying and selling securities, had done an "analysis of over two dozen studies that found an association between diverse boards and better financial performance and corporate governance."

While discussing the massive changes that have been happening in the workplace during the 2000s, a colleague reminisced about the start of her Executive MBA studies and how that is analogous to corporate leadership. One of her earliest memories of her MBA experience was each student completing psychometric assessments so that groups could be created with representation from each "type" of person. The rationale was that each group could only have a "whole brain" if each of the parts of the brain was represented by the members. If one perspective, approach, or style of thinking was missing, the group would be incomplete and vulnerable to making mistakes. Their goal, even before classes started, was to avoid blind spots and try to see around corners.

Modern organizations that are determined to remain viable regardless of the curve balls that are thrown at them know that they need to pay attention to issues like governance, risk management, and accountability. This is easier to do when companies/organizations have a 360-degree perspective and can avoid blind spots by taking the "whole-brain" approach. This plays out by hiring and appointing people based on what they can contribute, not how much they look like the people who are already sitting at the table. Some problems are only understood – and solvable – by people with the right combination of hard and soft skills, intelligence, and relevant lived experience.

In December 2020, CNN[13] reported that Nasdaq was proposing a rule that would require some evidence of diversity on the boards of directors of companies listed on the exchange. At the time when I was writing this book, this rule still needed

> the approval of the Securities and Exchange Commission to take effect, [and] would require companies to have at least two diverse directors, including one woman and one member of an 'underrepresented' minority group, including Black people, Latinos or

members of the LGBTQ2+ community. Smaller companies and foreign companies on the exchange could comply with two women directors.

(As reported by CNN[14] in December 2020)

This proposed rule is consistent with what has already been in place with Goldman Sachs' clients and for companies based in California. In January 2020, Goldman Sachs announced that it would not take a company public unless it has at least one diverse board member. For now, however, Goldman Sachs' version of diversity is focused on women, not BIPOC/BAME leaders. Since September 2020, the boards of all publicly traded companies based in California must have at least one minority member on them. Throughout 2020, Goldman Sachs[15] "built up a business to help recruit directors for those boards, which has expanded to cover public companies as well." Banks are very intentional, "it's a sign that there are not just morals at play – there is money at stake, too." So once again, it's easy to make the moral and practical/financial argument in favor of diversity, and ideally inclusion.

IDENTITIES AND THE FUTURE

I am not sure what is worse, when employers and colleagues buy into the mythology and false narrative that diverse candidates and employees are less qualified than white ones or when diverse candidates internalize these stereotypes and start to believe them. In my opinion, both are terrible. I do hope that the growing acknowledgment of the dire mental health consequences (e.g., trauma) associated with discrimination and exclusion should be an additional signal to people in underrepresented groups who have been working in survival mode and who have been isolated and gaslit, to start seeing things differently.

It is possible that when many BIPOC/BAME people started their careers they were treated well while they were still in junior roles. Then, slowly, over time, they may have started to experience more frequent subtle or not so subtle microaggressions, exclusion, and minor disappointments when they were denied opportunities for career-building assignments or promotions. In some ways, this may have been analogous to the proverbial frog in a pot of water. When the frog starts out, the water is a comfortable temperature. But, over time, as the temperature gets slightly warmer, then warmer, and warmer still, the dangerously hot temperature is not perceptible until it is too late. Likewise, when low-key but persistent bigotry happens over time, racialized people may remain practical and focus on doing their work, and taking care of themselves and their families, while the impact of the ongoing mistreatment starts to compound and intensify. It can be tough to know how bad an environment is until you get away from it for long enough to see what it feels like to be welcomed and appreciated for who you are and what you can contribute.

The mental gymnastics that BIPOC, LBGTQ2+, differently-abled, and other members of equity-seeking groups, must use to function within non-progressive and unwelcoming work environments eventually becomes exhausting. At the same time, we can learn from the Organization for Economic Co-operation and Development's (OECD) 2016 report, *The State of the North American Labor Market*,[16] which predicts that the average age of Canadians is expected to get much higher with the ratio of the elderly to the working-age people to nearly double over the next 20 years. The demographic patterns in the United States[17] are similar. The growing recognition of and the unwillingness to suffer from the damage caused by discrimination and exclusion in the workplace plus the anticipated demographic changes (whereby the vacancies left by retiring employees can't be filled by smaller younger generations) should result in more competition for employees. I predict that progressive employers will win the competition for talent in the long term. My sincere hope is that one of the outcomes of the ongoing reckoning around systemic and individual racism is that those who have been "othered" because of their identities start to get the credit and respect that they deserve. Equally important, my hope is that they start to feel more confident in their abilities because of what they have accomplished despite the obstacles.

NOTES

1 Smith, C., & Yoshino, K. (2019). *Uncovering talent a new model of inclusion*. Deloitte. www2.deloitte.com/content/dam/Deloitte/us/Documents/about-deloitte/us-about-deloitte-uncovering-talent-a-new-model-of-inclusion.pdf

2 Goffman, E. (1963). *Stigma: Notes on the management of spoiled identity*. Simon & Schuster, p. 102.

3 DeAngelis, T. (2019, February). The legacy of trauma. *Monitor on Psychology, 50*(2). www.apa.org/monitor/2019/02/legacy-trauma

4 Perry, B. D., & Winfrey, O. (2021). *What happened to you?: Conversations on trauma, resilience, and healing*. Flatiron Books. https://us.macmillan.com/books/9781250223210/whathappenedtoyou

5 Smith, C., & Yoshino, K. (2019). *Uncovering talent a new model of inclusion*. Deloitte. www2.deloitte.com/content/dam/Deloitte/us/Documents/about-deloitte/us-about-deloitte-uncovering-talent-a-new-model-of-inclusion.pdf

6 Brown, J. (2016) *Inclusion: Diversity, the new workplace & the will to change*. Advantage Media Group. https://jenniferbrownspeaks.com/inclusion-book

7 *Canadian Charter of Rights and Freedoms*, s 15, Part I of the Constitution Act, 1982, being Schedule B to the Canada Act 1982 (UK), 1982, c11 https://laws-lois.justice.gc.ca/eng/const/page-15.html

8 Deschamps, T. (2019, July 24). Canadian people of colour carry an 'emotional tax' at work. *The Hamilton Spectator*. www.thespec.com/business/2019/07/24/canadian-people-of-colour-carry-an-emotional-tax-at-work.html

9 Jana, T. (2021, September 24). *How to lose a chief diversity officer in 6 months. Medium*. https://index.medium.com/how-to-lose-a-chief-diversity-officer-in-6-months-6db0dfba6169

10 Sneader, K., Yee, L. (2019, January). One is the loneliest number. *McKinsey Quarterly*. www.mckinsey.com/featured-insights/gender-equality/one-is-the-loneliest-number

11 Powers, L. (2015, October 2). *Tories pledge new RCMP Tip Line to report forced marriage and other 'barbaric* practices'. CBC News. www.cbc.ca/news/politics/canada-election-2015-barbaric-cultural-practices-law-1.3254118

12 Posner, C. (2020, December 2). *Blog: Nasdaq proposes a "comply or explain" Board diversity mandate*. JD Supra. www.jdsupra.com/legalnews/blog-nasdaq-proposes-a-comply-or-29494/

13 Isidore, C. (2020, December 2). *Nasdaq to corporate America: Make your boards more diverse or get out*. CNN. www.cnn.com/2020/12/01/investing/nasdaq-rule-board-of-directors-diversity/index.html

14 Isidore, C. (2020, December 2). *Nasdaq to corporate America: Make your boards more diverse or get out*. CNN. www.cnn.com/2020/12/01/investing/nasdaq-rule-board-of-directors-diversity/index.html

15 Hirsch, L. (2021, January 23). The business case for boardroom diversity. *The New York Times*. www-nytimes-com.cdn.amp-project.org/c/s/www.nytimes.com/2021/01/23/business/dealbook/diversity-board-directors.amp.html

16 Broecke, S., Singh, S., & Swaim, P. (2016, June). *The state of the North American labour market*. OECD. www.oecd.org/unitedstates/The-state-of-the-north-american-labour-market-june-2016.pdf

17 Rogers, L., & Wilder, K. (2020, June 25). *Shift in working-age population relative to older and younger Americans*. Census.gov. www.census.gov/library/stories/2020/06/working-age-population-not-keeping-pace-with-growth-in-older-americans.html

CHAPTER 8

The Importance of Networking, Mentorship ... and Diligence

Based on everything that I've been seeing in my practice and learning about from other sources, very few people should expect to spend their entire career in one role or within one organization. This implies that it's imperative that employees understand the importance of networking and mentorship – and diligently use both strategies. In this chapter, I explain my rationale for this perspective and offer guidance on the proactive steps that all employees should take to support their ongoing progress and success.

The hard truth is that in the workplace some people feel as if they do not fit in and/or they are excluded on some level(s) due to their identity. As a result, they are likely to have weaker networks. And being poorly connected can hinder career mobility and keep you underemployed and plateaued.

I've had countless corporate professionals and government employees tell me they don't bother with networking. They say they don't want to use their time that way since they're so busy doing their work. They argue that networking is less important for them because they already have a secure job.

One misconception about networking is that it's about attending networking or social events and rushing around having conversations trying to impress others by explaining what you do and why you or your product/service is the best. It's not enjoyable to be on the receiving end of those interactions and you won't get very far if you're known or remembered for being "that guy" or "that woman" who would not stop talking about themselves or their interests. Similarly, networking is more than "working the room" to

    DOI: 10.4324/9781003328988-9

collect the maximum number of business cards at an event. Neither approach sets the stage for making the kind of first impression that will translate into something that is positive and sustainable in the long term.

In my opinion, networking is about establishing a real connection that you can follow up on and nurture over time into a meaningful and mutually beneficial professional relationship. The key takeaways are that it should be sincere and set the foundation for a win–win situation. Take an interest in others and most of the time they will return the favor (that is the law of reciprocity). I believe that everyone knows something, and everyone knows someone. Usually, with a little bit of effort, you can be of some assistance or support to many of the people with whom you interact.

LARGE MANDATES CAN'T BE HANDLED SOLO

From everything that I've experienced or seen up close, as you climb the ranks in an organization, your level of responsibility expands, yet your span of control diminishes. You become responsible for a broader range of deliverables or outcomes, and more employees. You also become more dependent on the work of others to achieve your objectives. As you climb the hierarchy or corporate ladder, your success comes to rely on other people's success and their ability to deliver.

In practice, there are countless situations where your ability to speak with someone to get context, help, or favors is essential. This is especially true when timelines are tight, or the work is unfamiliar. This is why the conversations and interactions that managers and leaders have with their colleagues, peers, and subordinates determine their results and long-term success.

Over the years, I've seen how people who are better connected are much more successful – regardless of their actual skill, talent, work ethic, or qualifications. Of course, having plenty of those never hurts. But the most successful people

I know have kept on with their networking and kept up with their contacts. Here are some simple but effective ways to improve your network.

Go Deep, Not Wide

Time and energy permitting, try to connect with people you already know. Many of us have social media connections whom we don't see often or have never met. It may be too hard to rely on meeting new people and establishing new relationships in this hybrid and digital era so try to keep in touch with your existing network. Likewise, for people with whom you have an existing offline relationship, as a starting point, keep in touch with them to enjoy and deepen those bonds. Odds are good that, over time, those relationships will lead to additional relationships.

Try to Have Some Visibility

Pre-pandemic, we would see certain people periodically in real life. That made it easier to keep in touch and stay top of mind. Liking, commenting, and sharing other people's social media posts is almost like passing someone on the sidewalk or in the hallway. These digital interactions give you visibility with the people to whom you are connected to online. Now that it is harder to spontaneously run into people since many have transitioned to hybrid or remote work and generally may be keeping tighter social circles, try to avoid being invisible. With so much uncertainty out there in the economy and the job market, this is not a good time to be completely off the grid.

Join in Online

Consider participating in online events or joining an online group or cause to establish a foundation for new relationships. In the past, when all meetings were in person, it took more effort to attend. Now, most board meetings and volunteering are happening online. This could be a way to learn new things, reinforce skills, and get to know new people. Consider doing something that is closely aligned with your interests, or you could try something quite different to be exposed to new ideas and new people.

Build Career Resilience through Your Network

Whether you are looking for work or you are a long-term employee, networking is crucial to success. In the context of work, it's essential that you have people who are willing and able to vouch for you when jobs become available and when there are opportunities for new projects, assignments, promotions, etc. These same people are likely to want to help you if your employment situation ever takes a turn for the worse and you find yourself needing to find a new role.

Likewise, in the business, freelance, and "side hustle" world, it is easier for people to refer a potential client or customer to you when they know that they will receive excellent service and results from you. This confidence only comes after you have demonstrated that you can deliver as promised. This implies that you have had an ongoing relationship.

Isolation Makes You Vulnerable

Out in the wild, a lone animal is more vulnerable to attack ... and in the schoolyard, the loner has nobody to watch his or her back. Likewise, workplace friendships can protect you from bullying, harassment, and alienation. There is strength in numbers so when you are part of the group, you're harder to attack.

In so many ways, having a network builds some resilience into your career and professional circumstances. To some extent, it is not what you know but who you know. In addition, it's not only who you know, but who knows you.

Learn How to Network

Networking is a skill. Some people are naturally great at it. Others find it stressful. If you're not a natural networker, you can learn. Here are a few pointers about networking to help you get started.

Find the right group. Not every networking group or context is a good fit. When you find the right group or environment, you will quickly find yourself feeling more at ease. If you attend a networking event and come away feeling like it was not a good match, try another. I have seen certain people volunteer in various capacities as a way to do some very structured networking. By volunteering for an organization with a mandate that they're interested in, they get to interact with (i.e., network) with people with whom they have shared interests while engaging in something that has some meaning and a pro-social outcome.

Be yourself. In terms of the mechanics of networking, in principle, I think it is best to be yourself. In your other relationships, you probably follow the normal rules of honesty, integrity, sincerity, and decency. These are great qualities to bring to your networking relationships. Also, when you act like yourself while developing new relationships, as people get to know you, there will be consistency. If you act one way during the initial interactions but a different way later, people will be confused and wonder which "you" is the real you. More importantly, that lack of consistency may be quite off-putting and counterproductive.

Set a small goal for events. Instead of going into an event imagining you're going to somehow "work the room" or the "digital breakout room," aim to talk to just one person, in a meaningful way.

Follow up promptly and directly. After meeting with someone for the first time, follow up once with a quick note via email or send an invitation, including a brief message, to connect via LinkedIn. Most people do not bother to follow up, so if you're one of the rare ones who do, within 24 hours of the meeting, it may help you stand out favorably.

Don't Wait. The best time to network is now. Do not wait until something goes badly and you really need to network to find a new job (or to help grow your business). Building mutually beneficial relationships takes time.

Create a Diverse Network. Simply being part of an open network instead of a closed one is the best predictor of career success. When you are part of a narrowly focused, closed network (e.g., a teacher who only interacts with other teachers), you repeatedly hear the same ideas, which reaffirm what you already know and believe. This is what happens when you build a network that is full of people who are the same as you. In contrast, when you are part of a diverse, broad, and open network, you become part of multiple groups. This means that you can have various unique relationships, experiences, and knowledge that other people in closed or narrowly focused groups do not have.

MENTORSHIP: A PREDICTOR OF SUCCESS

Mentorship is one of the predictors of success. Given the attention that's been focused on systemic racism and discrimination since summer 2020, unfortunately, it's become clearer that certain people, including BIPOC/BAME, people with disabilities, religious minorities, and members of the LBGTQ2+ community are less likely to have access to mentors to the same extent that their straight, white able-bodied colleagues do.

During the summer of 2018, I was asked to talk about the benefits of working with a coach, and the value of mentorship as part of a person's career/business strategic planning at an evening event of networking, learning, and inspiration for young tech entrepreneurs.

I was happy to give the talk. Although these remarks were made to a young audience of high school and university students, the ideas apply to a broader audience, so I have summarized those thoughts in writing and expanded upon them here.

HARD KNOCK (BUSINESS) LIFE

Anyone who has been following me on social media or reading my blog over the years knows that I am an advocate for self-employment and entrepreneurship, since both of these styles of work lead to long-term autonomy and resilience.

My brother sometimes reminds me of something that one of our maternal uncles used to say when we were growing up over 30 years ago: *"Whatever you do, make it your business,"* he'd say, in his deep voice with a super-cool Jamaican accent. He was ahead of his time with his idea about doing what you are good at and enjoying it, knowing that the money would follow. He also appreciated the value of remaining in control of one's destiny and livelihood.

In my opinion, it's exciting and impressive to start or run your own business, at any age. But when you're in high school or university, you don't have as much education from the school of hard knocks as older entrepreneurs do. This means that you have your work cut out for you. Similarly, when you are in the earlier stages of your career, there are lots of hidden obstacles that you only see in hindsight.

Thankfully, you really don't have to learn everything the hard way. That is a dangerous and expensive way to learn and grow a business or make progress in your career. It is much smarter, safer, and cheaper to learn as much as you can from others.

MENTORSHIP IS FOR PROTÉGÉS

Some people are reluctant to ask for help because they think it's a sign of weakness. In the world of entrepreneurship (and many workplaces), weakness is a quality that most people avoid. But I don't consider participation in mentorship a weakness. Here's why. In any mentorship relationship, there's a mentor and a *mentee or protégé.* I prefer the term protégé because protégés are known for their talent and potential.

According to Walter Isaacson's 2011 biography of Steve Jobs,[1] Jobs had seven mentors. When I first learned this, I found it surprising, since Jobs had a reputation for being an independent thinking "tech cowboy."

The folklore around Jobs was that he did what he thought was appropriate regardless of what others said or the trends of the day. The reality was different. He had several mentors for different stages and aspects of his life. One of his mentors was Robert Friedland whom he met while auditing university courses. Friedland taught Jobs about selling and persuasion, two skills that Jobs mastered and used throughout his life. Friedland also owned an apple orchard – that influence is obvious.

According to Isaacson, Bob Noyce was another of Jobs' mentors. Noyce is credited with inventing the microchip and giving Jobs a tremendous insider's perspective in the early days of the tech industry. A third mentor was a Zen Master named Kobun Chino Otagawa who officiated at Jobs' wedding. A more public and pervasive example of Otagawa's impact is the minimalist design aesthetic that's now one of the qualities for which Apple is known.

Clearly, the impact of these mentors is seen all over the business strategy that was so vital to the success of Apple. What is also clear to me is that, although much of the mythology around Jobs is his independent-tech-cowboy reputation for doing what he liked and not following others, he was influenced by his mentors.

Eventually, later in his career, Jobs evolved from being the protégé who received advice from several mentors to becoming a mentor to Mark Zuckerberg, the founder of Facebook, and Sergey Brin and Larry Page, the co-founders of Google.

One takeaway idea that comes from these examples of mentorship is that receiving mentorship should not be viewed as a sign of weakness. It should be seen as a predictor of greatness. So, whether you are just starting your career (or your business) or you have been at it for a while, find ways to learn from mentors, formally and informally. Like Jobs, we can all have multiple mentors, and we can learn something different from each of them.

ACTIONS SPEAK LOUDER THAN WORDS

A second message that I shared with the young tech entrepreneurs is a lesson that I learned from an incidental mentor whom I met early on in my journey as a self-employed person. He said:

"How you do something is how you do everything."

In other words, how you do one thing is an indication of how you do everything. For example, a typo in an email, blog post, report, or a printed letter can easily be interpreted as a sign of carelessness. Failing to call or send an email that you promised to send is a signal that you may be unreliable.

On the surface, this is unusual advice to share with young tech entrepreneurs – or in the context of career development. In the context of entrepreneurship, most people would focus on technology or business plans and overlook this important detail. Similarly, in the corporate setting, the focus might be on presence, knowledge, or technical excellence. In my experience, this simple advice is very impactful. Not understanding and executing on this one notion can undermine the success of your reputation, product, or service.

One of my most sincere hopes is that more organizations will find ways to facilitate mentorship for all employees who may have been overlooked in the past. From an equity perspective, that would be fair and just. Given the financial impact that the pandemic has had on so many industries, this is a smart time to welcome the best contributions from all employees. This means improving corporate cultures so that people do not need to cover at work, and they can focus on their work instead of self-protection. True inclusion may lead to productivity and outcomes that tips the scale in favor of success instead of failure.

For employees who have traditionally been neglected or passed over for opportunities because they were not white, straight, or able-bodied, etc. this is a good time to try again. No doubt there are still lots of employers who only pay lip service to inclusion, merit, and equal opportunity. Thankfully, that is offset by more employers than ever who believe in these values – and practice them – while they continue to innovate in a progressive, future-focused manner.

BUTTERING UP THE BOSS – FROM HOME

One of the classic inside jokes in countless workplaces is that almost everything gets discussed – and even decided – during smoke breaks, coffee, or drinks. The flatterer, the apple-polisher, the butt-kisser – there are so many terms of endearment for the boss's pet – has always experienced enviable career progression with the right type of boss. Anyone who has been working for a while has probably seen someone get ahead by buttering up the boss.

It's also easy to see how buttering up the boss is more effective when it's done in person. I mean, how practical is buttering up someone via group Zoom or Google Meet interactions? Flattery, giving small gifts, and countless other ways of ingratiating oneself are easier to accomplish through frequent face-to-face contact.

Pre-Covid-19, a lot of people could butter up the boss and get ahead. Now, with so many people working remotely or in a hybrid environment, opportunities for that "bootlicking" or ingratiation have become more difficult since there are fewer opportunities. Now, the "doers" – the quiet, humble, diligent employees who were often overlooked and who have been working hard from the beginning – may finally start to shine. With profit margins thinner during the pandemic and recovery, the people who contribute the most might start to get noticed and respected. This scenario far too often applies to racialized people who needed to be twice as good just to get their foot in the door. In the past, these doers have not been promoted because they were told that their contributions are too critical to the organization's mandate. Their work is appreciated and relied upon. Yet, they are dehumanized on some level since their desire to be rewarded for their efforts, permitted to reach their potential, and be respected enough to be given promotions are denied.

In my opinion, this is a time for hard-working, productive employees to be revealed and celebrated. Now is the time for these doers to step up and highlight how they are helping their organizations satisfy priorities and contribute to outcomes. The people who are the flittering and flattering types may not be able to show themselves in a very favorable light when productivity is now more transparent. There are fewer opportunities to smoke, eat, or drink with the boss and deflect responsibility.

Performance evaluations will let the quiet doers shine. The blinders should finally be off.

Whether you're a quiet doer or a flashy butterfly, here are *five general tips to stay visible when working remotely or in a hybrid environment*:

1. Communicate frequently with your manager (e.g., weekly bi-lateral briefings or meetings). The more he, they, or she knows about the work you're doing, the better.
2. Treat online meetings like you would any meeting. Show up on time, properly dressed and prepared.
3. Before your next meeting, turn on your video camera and take a look at your background. Does it need tidying up? With people working from home since March 2020, it may be tempting to relax a little. If there are tricycles, residue from snacks/meals, and dirty laundry in the frame, it's time to de-clutter your workspace – or finally figure out how to use the virtual background.
4. Here's a great opportunity to be seen – regularly arrive a few minutes early to video meetings and use that time to chat with colleagues. You might also get a chance to chat with the boss.
5. These days, knowledge is power. Sharing knowledge can be your superpower. If you know a great tech tool that might be useful to your coworkers, share what you

know. If you have discovered articles or other references that can help your colleague or even your boss – share them. This is a chance to develop your reputation as a go-to person when it comes to areas in which you are knowledgeable.

NOTE

1 Isaacson, W. (2011) *Steve Jobs*. Simon & Schuster, www.simonands-chuster.com/books/Steve-Jobs/Walter-Isaacson/9781982176860

CHAPTER 9

Workplace Scapegoats and the Glass Cliff

Although rarely discussed out in the open, highly capable people can become scapegoats and then need to figure out how to salvage their careers. In this chapter, I explain who is most likely to become a workplace scapegoat. I will also address a very nuanced version of scapegoating, the glass cliff, a concern for women and members of underrepresented groups. Scapegoating and the glass cliff scenario are among the most common problems that my clients present to me. In this chapter, I'll explain both of these types of stressful situations, how and why they happen, and how you can protect yourself.

It is well documented that in organizations that have a high percentage of diverse employees, the diversity usually exists on the lower rungs of the organization. As you climb the hierarchy, there is less or no diversity. For example, *The Society Pages*[1] reported that in 2020, 85.8% of the *Fortune* 500 CEOs were still white males even though men only make up 35% of the population. Only 1% of the Fortune 500 CEOs are African Americans, 2.4% are East Asians or South Asians, and 3.4% are Latinx.

What is less clear is the exact phenomena that are happening to keep certain people out. In this chapter, I will describe two specific things that may be part of the reason for limited representation at the higher levels within organizations: Scapegoating and the glass cliff.

Scapegoating and the glass cliff may sound like something made up or exaggerated by people who are paranoid or unwilling to accept responsibility for their failure. Unfortunately, for the victims and those who value fairness, these are legitimate phenomena.

DOI: 10.4324/9781003328988-10

SCAPEGOATS

Anyone who has worked within certain medium to large-sized organizations understands that they do not always operate in ways that are good for all employees – sometimes there are winners and there are losers.

More people are familiar with the word scapegoat than the term glass cliff. Scapegoat can be a noun or an adjective and it is what happens when someone is unfairly blamed when things go badly. To be scapegoated is an exceedingly difficult situation because often the scapegoat ends up out of a job or demoted, and their reputations take a hit.

It can be hard to know when you are becoming a scapegoat. Obviously, the person or people who are doing it will not announce it up front – if anything, they are likely to deny it or gaslight you. Here are some clues to watch for to help you know if you are becoming a scapegoat.

One signal to watch for is that your manager used to frequently seek you out for your advice and input, but now they behave as though you have never been their confidante or advisor. They only want to talk to you about your deliverables, dates, and various metrics. They are now all business. Another change to watch for is that your boss may start communicating with you by email instead of by voice, face-to-face/video communication, or, pre- and post-covid, in person. Their email messages are now terse. You get the feeling that the email messages might be blind copied to HR and/or your boss's boss.

You may notice that your manager gives you high-profile, high-risk assignments or projects but then will not talk to you about them. They will not give you guidance or feedback even when there are high-impact decisions to be made. They are remaining very "hands off" and setting you up to take the blame if the project or initiative fails. You may also learn that your boss gives you urgent work, but they also give the same assignments to other people – and do not tell you or your colleagues about the duplication. You only find out about it when you bump into a co-worker doing the same thing the boss also asked you to do.

Another telling sign is that you begin to get email messages from your boss about projects that have nothing to do with you. There are notes on these messages from your boss, like "Take care of this today!" Your boss is trying to tag you with missteps and problems that are completely unrelated to your job. If you are lucky, your co-workers will tell you that your manager has brought you up more than once in their presence – for example, to say "Check with Jessica on the status of that issue – and if she doesn't have a good answer, let me know!"

Sometimes the changes and warning signals are more about the way you feel when interacting with your boss. For example, when you are in the same room with your boss, you feel the tension in the air. You used to have an easy relationship with plenty of joking around and banter, but those days are over. Or, when you look back over the year(s) you've spent working with your boss, you remember the hours and hours of advising, support, and encouragement that you gave your boss just because you are a kind and cooperative person. Now your fearful manager regrets confiding in you and relying upon you. They wish they could take back all the fears and worries they expressed while with you. Since they can't take those conversations back, they want you to disappear. This all adds up to a gut instinct that tells you, "I am being set up by my manager."

If you have seen some of the signs that you're probably being scapegoated, here are some suggestions on *what to do next*:

Get your own legal advice immediately. Refuse to rely on in-house counsel or an outside law firm that represents your employer, if offered. Your company's lawyer is not your lawyer, and you are not their client. Seeking advice early may preserve more of your options. Waiting to see how things play out may reduce your options. Also, be careful about relying too much on your union if you're part of one. A union can't place your interests above the interests of another union member since you are both equal members who, in principle, are also entitled to the union's support.

Use a lawyer to guide you through the process of wrongful dismissal (or other options). If things escalate to the point that you are fired for reasons that are not linked to your job performance then you might consider seeking legal advice to deal with wrongful dismissal. This will help to repair some of the damage that your reputation has suffered. Ideally, this process may also provide you with some severance money that will help to sustain you until you find a new job. Try not to waste time proving your innocence (that's your lawyer's job); instead, focus on getting back to work.

Seek nuanced counsel if "intersecting" issues are at play. If sexual harassment, workplace bullying, or discrimination based on your race, ethnicity, sexual orientation/identity, etc. are contributing factors, I strongly suggest that you interview a few lawyers or ask around for a recommendation. Some lawyers simply don't appreciate these nuanced types of harassment and their impact on people who are in marginalized groups because of their identity. When your lawyer does not understand these issues, they are less likely to be able to represent you adequately because they won't fully appreciate the traumatic implications of what you've been through.

Consider some counselling or therapy. This type of support should help you restore your self-confidence and process other emotions. To put it politely, being made into a scapegoat is traumatic and complicated. You'll benefit tremendously from some help to get you recalibrated so that you can show up well rather than damaged at your next job – and during any interviews that lead to that job.

Sign up for outplacement or career coaching. Equally important and urgent is some reliable career advice and related support that will provide you with the strategies and assistance that you need to line up your next job. Ideally, your former employer will cover the costs of the outplacement/career coaching as part of your severance and wrongful dismissal package.

These scapegoating situations often fly under the radar. One reason why these scenarios can hide in plain sight is because of the use of non-disclosure agreements (NDAs). When someone is scapegoated, if they understand their rights, they will negotiate a settlement that includes severance pay and damages. Invariably, in order to receive these payments, the scapegoat needs to agree to not disclose the details surrounding their departure. Since the victims do not usually talk about what happened, unless it involves a public figure, it stays rather low-profile. This is also true when discussing glass cliff situations; however, the glass cliff is experienced primarily by women and racial/ethnic minorities.

THE GLASS CLIFF AND CAREER DERAILMENT

Career derailment happens when someone, usually in a leadership position, is perceived as a poor fit for the challenges they face on the job. When a leader's career derails, it means he or she will not be considered for promotions because of their real or perceived diminished effectiveness. Although some derailed managers are fired from their jobs, many remain employed but are no longer seen as promotable to higher-level positions.

Unfortunately, executive derailment is very common. It happens to 30% to 50% of all high-functioning leaders at some point in their career. Further, since 50% of employees say that they have left a job because of their manager, a lot of managers are under-performing. Clearly, there's a real need for executive and leadership coaching, particularly during the earlier phases of a leader's career.

Despite these grim statistics, not all instances of derailment are the leader's fault. In fact, sometimes candidates for leadership positions are put into high-risk situations that are almost predestined to fail. When we look carefully at the details of many of these derailment scenarios, we can see certain common characteristics. There is an even more nuanced and specific form of career derailment and it's called the glass cliff.

The term "glass cliff" was first coined by psychology researchers Michelle Ryan and Alexander Haslam in 2005.[2] The phrase intentionally plays off the better-known term "glass ceiling," which is used to describe the challenges that women and other underrepresented groups face as they try to advance professionally.

Ryan and Haslam argue that women and other members of equity-seeking groups often take on leadership roles under very different circumstances than men. Basically, the glass cliff phenomenon predicts that women and other members of underrepresented groups are more likely to be appointed to riskier leadership positions that are associated with a higher rate of failure. These leadership positions are more precarious than other (male-dominated) leadership positions.

A public example of the glass cliff is when (former) UK Prime Minister Teresa May attempted to implement a "Brexit" strategy for her country. Although I am not a true political pundit, from my perspective, it was clear that May had been in politics for a long time and had never had an opportunity to become the Prime Minister. Her male counterparts who knew that they could always make a play for the top job did not want to take the role when the odds of failure were so high. On the other hand, May knew that under "normal" circumstances she did not have a good chance of taking on the Prime Minister role. Further, her party might have preferred that she become Prime Minister during the turbulent time, and then, when she failed, she could be replaced.

Ryan and Haslam (2005) note that during tumultuous times, women and minorities are often chosen as leaders. This is often because an organization (or a country) is looking for something or someone novel to represent a bold, new direction that will help it regain its footing. The symbolism is important because it's consistent with the stereotype that women are usually comforting and nurturing during difficult times.

Despite the official rules and policies that may be in place, your gender, racial, and other aspects of your identity can have an impact on the types of roles that you're offered.

Within certain government organizations, promotions are based on competitive selection processes, so in principle, they should be less vulnerable to this minefield of complex negative forces. In practice, however, in most organizations, there are places where bias can seep in. For instance, diverse candidates may be among the few candidates who make it onto the shortlist of people being considered for the position. At that point, when the hiring manager/committee is given the discretion to appoint the person who they think is the best fit for the role, often the candidate who matches the people already working there – or who will fit in the best – is chosen. In more progressive and just organizations, people are chosen based on what they can contribute.

Although these glass cliff roles are easy to see and classify as risky, women, people of color, and members of other underrepresented groups often accept these promotions because they have far fewer leadership opportunities. They step into these roles and take a deliberate and calculated risk with the expectation that it will help their careers.

Unfortunately, from the beginning, the deck is stacked against them. They soon find they're unable to gain access to the support that they'll need to beat the odds. Examples of this lack of support are discussed in this March 2019 article: "The 'Glass Cliff' Puts Women in Power During Crisis – Often Without Support."[3]

On the other hand, men are more comfortable turning these jobs down because they are fairly confident that they are likely to get a better opportunity if they can wait it out a little. Women and members of other underrepresented groups often cannot afford to do the same (PBS, April 2019[4]). When these female or minority leaders fail, odds are very good that a man will step in to fix the situation and tie up loose ends. This scenario also has a name – it's called the savior effect.

When a woman has had the chance to resolve a crisis and is perceived to have failed, corporate board members (or voters) are more likely to choose what they see as the safe option to replace the failed leader: A white man. This has played out publicly at Yahoo!, Toys R Us, Lucent Technologies, Hewlett-Packard, and many other organizations as described in this 2014 article from *The Guardian*[5] which provides more details and references about the savior effect.

Even though there's some systemic unfairness that's built in to most of these circumstances, the fact that there are more men in the leadership pipeline also means that they're more likely to become the savior based on statistics alone.

OVERCOMING DERAILMENT AND/OR THE GLASS CLIFF

When complex, risky, high visibility, under-resourced, and high-stakes leadership opportunities emerge – and are offered to unsuspecting candidates – it would be great if more leaders saw what was happening, intervened, and made things right. For instance, the person who is in the glass cliff situation could be offered the resources they need to build a strong team, given access to executive coaching, and the written promise of a golden parachute if things end poorly and a generous bonus if they are successful. Unfortunately, that is not how things usually play out in real life.

The hard truth is that if you find yourself in this situation, and there's no time to build a stronger team or hire a skilled and experienced executive coach, you'd be wise to start preparing yourself to find a new job. You will need to discretely begin asking your contacts if they can make any introductions on your behalf that may lead to discussions about emerging comparable career opportunities. In addition, you should also be ready to negotiate with the person trying to throw you under the bus if they try to put you on probation or a performance improvement plan (PIP). It's such a tumultuous time that I'd also suggest that you keep dated notes of what's happened and continues to happen. My preferred way to do this is to send these notes to yourself via personal email so that they are date-stamped and easy to share with a lawyer if needed. I also strongly suggest that you get independent legal advice from an employment lawyer who understands the human rights angles. Early legal advice and/or intervention will help you preserve your options and avoid getting pushed into a corner.

Once your lawyer has been retained and briefed, you're in a stronger position since they will support your negotiations with the person who is scapegoating you or pushing you off the glass cliff. You'll be better prepared to consider your severance package and exit strategy.

If necessary, and with your lawyer's blessing, go over the head of the person scapegoating you or pushing you off the glass cliff to the higher-up leaders and tell them the whole story. As a rule, people who are panicking and trying to blame others (e.g., bullies) don't like or want conflict. They want to scare you into doing what *they* want. Make them rationalize/explain. Get your severance package (or assignment out into a new role in the organization) ... and consider getting your employment lawyer to review your offer.

The glass cliff is probably one of the most difficult professional challenges that you can face since it happens when you have reached a high point in your career and it is often public. The fact that it happens when you thought you were starting to peak means that something that you were looking forward to as a career highlight turns into a career-limiting or possibly a career-ending move. Ouch. Also, it is bad enough to experience a setback but when it is visible or public, it feels so much worse.

Although it is almost impossible to anticipate all the potential twists and turns that could accompany such a complex situation, here are some *tips that should help you avoid some of the worst aspects associated with the glass cliff phenomenon.*

- When you're evaluating a new career opportunity, do your homework. This includes reading as much as you can about the organization, the industry, and the people involved. Ideally, this will also include some more nuanced research where you speak with people who should understand the role, mandate, backstory, context, hidden risks, challenges, etc. so that you can accurately evaluate your risks up front. When you know what you're likely to face, you can make a more informed decision rather than being blind-sided later, after it's too late to back out gracefully.

- Now that you have a clearer understanding of the risks, you will need to work around them by including these risks in your salary and in your bonus structure negotiations. Just like in other investments, the higher the risk, the higher the reward.
- Define success upfront by getting the Board, or whoever you will be reporting to, to set the performance standards (or co-establish the performance standards). Once the criteria that you'll be evaluated against have been set, then you can decide whether or not the expectations are achievable.
- Ask trusted colleagues, mentors, or corporate allies for their insights when you are considering a promotion. This is yet another reason why it is important to have a network in place before you need one. When you are dealing with something like this, you will need to be able to count on people with whom you have an established and high-trust relationship.
- Do not be afraid to walk away. Ousted women and members of equity-seeking groups do not normally get a second chance after they have fallen off, or to be more accurate, after they have been pushed off a glass cliff.
- Whether you're dealing with scapegoating, a glass cliff, or the less dramatic career derailers, if you can gain access to a corporate mentorship program, sign right up. You have little to lose and everything to gain. In the absence of a structured mentorship program, try to find a mentor, ally, or sponsor. Usually, mentors are more established than you but sometimes our peers may be suitable mentors if they understand things that you have not yet mastered.
- Try to find an ally and/or a sponsor. An ally is normally someone who is part of the mainstream (e.g., non-racialized, straight, cis-gendered, etc.) or who has more influence and/or status than you have and who may have access to networks, opportunities, or information that are

often denied to outsiders (e.g., BIPOC/BAME people, members of the LGBTQ2+ communities, people with disabilities, etc.). When an ally is willing and able to share resources, information, or introductions, it can change everything. A sponsor is anyone who has the ability to vouch for you, make introductions, create development-oriented opportunities for you, or make referrals that help you to make progress in your career. There's a reason why some people are successful – they have mentors, sponsors, and sometimes allies who are willing and able to light a path for them.

- Do not overlook the value of reading (or listening to) books written by people who have written about their experiences and benefit from what they learned. Often the insights that you can gain from those resources are equally or even more valuable than what you can learn from people within your circle.
- As I've mentioned before, it's always worth finding ways to build, improve, and expand your network.

Unsurprisingly, Michelle Ryan, Professor of Social and Organizational Psychology (and one of the original glass cliff researchers), argues that the combination of economic hardship from the coronavirus pandemic combined with the push for diversity, means that people of color (and women) are more likely to be set up on this glass cliff than may have been likely pre-pandemic. To offset these risks, companies need to make sure that women and people of color who are chosen for leadership positions get the support they need to remain successful. Further, responsible leaders need to ensure that their diversity, equity, and inclusion efforts don't stop at the appointment of a woman or BIPOC person to the C-suite.

I agree with Professor Ryan that the sad reality is that, if women and BIPOC/BAME candidates don't embrace opportunities, it might be a while before another one emerges. For every 100 men who were promoted to management from 2018 to 2019, only 68 Latina women were promoted. That number was even less for Black women, at 58, according to research by McKinsey & Company and LeanIn.org.[6] What's worse is that you can count the number of Black Fortune 500 CEOs on one hand, and none of them are women.

Now that you're armed with this context and knowledge, I hope that you'll be better prepared to advocate for the support you need as a leader – or better prepared to offer support to someone who's dealing with this scenario. Many leaders who are "in the know" understand that they can gain access to extremely valuable executive coaching and leadership development – paid for by their employer. It's only the isolated leaders who don't appreciate what may be possible or who try to go it alone.

ADDITIONAL RESOURCES

Since January 2019, I have been curating a list of resources (e.g., articles, books, websites, podcasts/videos, films etc.) that are designed to support racialized employees who face the double whammy of additional work-related challenges and fewer sources of support and guidance to deal with those problems. Although this information lives on my website, I'll make it easier to find by sharing the URL here: https://ioadvisory.com/career-professional-development-resources-fbec-members/[7]

NOTES

1 Zweigenhaft, R., & Dana, C. A. (2020, October 28). Fortune 500 CEOS, 2000–2020: Still male, still white. *The Society Pages*. Retrieved from https://thesocietypages.org/specials/fortune-500-ceos-2000-2020-still-male-still-white/
2 Ryan, M. K., & Haslam, S. A. (2005). The Glass Cliff: Evidence that Women are Over-Represented in Precarious Leadership Positions. *British Journal of Management*, 16(2), 81–90. https://psycnet.apa.org/record/2005-06147-001
3 Tong, T. (2019, March 28). The "glass cliff" puts women in power during crisis – often without support. *The World*. www.pri.org/stories/2019-03-28/glass-cliff-puts-women-power-during-crisis-often-without-support
4 Rohrich, Z. (2019, April 1). *How Brexit became a "glass cliff" for Theresa May*. PBS. www.pbs.org/newshour/world/how-brexit-became-a-glass-cliff-for-theresa-may

5 McCullough, D. G. (2014, August 8). Women CEOS: Why companies in crisis hire minorities – and then fire them. *The Guardian.* www.theguardian.com/sustainable-business/2014/aug/05/ fortune-500-companies-crisis-woman-ceo-yahoo-xerox-jc-penny-economy

6 LeanIn.Org and McKinsey & Company (2020, August 13). *The state of Black Women in corporate America.* Lean In and Mckinsey & Company https://media.sgff.io/sgff_r1eHetbDYb/ 2020-08-13/1597343917539/Lean_In_-_State_of_Black_Women_ in_Corporate_America_Report_1.pdf

7 https://ioadvisory.com/blog/

CHAPTER 10

Avoiding and Coping with Burnout at Work

Experiencing the types of career derailers addressed in this book definitely predisposes people who are trying to recover from these experiences to develop burnout. Consequently, in an effort to be comprehensive, in this chapter, I will share information and guidance on avoiding and coping with burnout.

Remember when the summer holidays inspired you as a kid to throw your school papers carelessly in the air while trading in your backpack for a beach towel, ball, or racquet? Those were the days, right?

Years ago, I was speaking with Melissa, my part-time proofreader and editor who sometimes suggests potential blog topics. She commented on the fatigue or burnout that sometimes hits her during the summer. For her, this exhaustion is due to attending numerous weddings, keeping her young daughter entertained while continuing to get her own work done – plus the sometimes-oppressive heat and humidity. For me, summer sometimes gets tiring because of ongoing business development and content development for fall/winter projects, plus ongoing client-facing work.

For most adults, summer does not necessarily mean a break. And, although it remains a popular season for people to book time off for a staycation or vacation, I think it's still safe to assume that those sun-filled months don't always imply fun and relaxation. In fact, over the years, I've seen a common trend where many professionals experience some form of burnout during the summer, either feeling distracted, unmotivated, overwhelmed, or a combination of these states. Of course, this isn't actually caused by hot weather or the prevalence of Hawaiian shirts, patio parties, or umbrellas in our drinks. So, why, in the midst of these better times, do people report feeling burned out when the calendar gets closer to July and August?

Often, summer's rise in temperature matches the increased need to perform a balancing act between work and greater demands in our personal lives. This burden goes beyond the hassle of juggling to make it to your cousin's summer solstice-themed wedding while writing a report for your boss; although, I do believe this is where a lot of summer burnout begins. All at once, people with demanding professions are expected to attend a greater number of social and family events, and yet, still maintain their work efficiency. Suddenly, the kids are out of school and depending on their age(s), you'll need to find proper supervision, either in camps or daycare. You might also start dreading the mail, which may include a smattering of summer engagement and wedding invitations. Not to mention the pressure to book a cottage or camping excursion before the leaves change color and it's too cold to swim. It's no wonder so many are exhausted when they're expected to put in the same number of hours in their work-week while doing these extra activities. And what is additionally stressful is the unspoken assumption that we should all appear happy about it because … hey, it's summer! Unfortunately, not everyone can manage the multitasking of "extra" fun without feeling overwhelmed by the added demands on their time.

Of course, burnout can happen at any time of the year, regardless of the season. Burnout is a state of chronic stress that may lead to physical and emotional exhaustion, cynicism and detachment, feelings of ineffectiveness, and a lack of motivation. In many cases, you're so busy that you become burned out before you know it; you miss the symptoms and therefore you aren't able to heed the early warnings and turn things around before burnout takes hold.

THE SIGNS OF BURNOUT

Chronic exhaustion or fatigue. In the early stages of burnout, you may feel lackluster and experience a lack of energy and feel tired most days. In the latter stages, you feel physically and emotionally drained, depleted, and exhausted, and you may feel a sense of dread about whatever lies ahead on any given day.

Insomnia. In the early phases of burnout, you may have trouble falling asleep or staying asleep one or two nights a week. In the latter stages, insomnia may become a chronic, nightly ordeal. Despite how exhausted you are, you just can't sleep.

Forgetfulness and inability to concentrate and focus. A lack of focus and mild forgetfulness are early signs. Later, as your burnout progresses, the problems may get to the point where you can't get your work done and everything starts to pile up.

Physical symptoms. Physical symptoms may include headaches, heart palpitations, shortness of breath, chest pain, gastrointestinal pain, dizziness, and/or fainting (all of which should be medically assessed to rule out other causes).

Increased illness. Since your body is now depleted, your immune system is weaker and this makes you more vulnerable to infections, colds, flu, and other immune-related medical problems.

Loss of appetite. In the early stages of burnout, you may not feel hungry and may end up skipping a few meals. As your burnout progresses, you may lose your appetite altogether and start to lose a significant amount of weight.

Anxiety. In the beginning, you may experience mild symptoms of tension, worry, and edginess. As you move closer to full-blown burnout, your anxiety may become so serious that it interferes with your ability to work productively and may cause problems in your personal life.

Depression. In the earlier stages of burnout, you may feel a bit sad and occasionally hopeless, in addition to some feelings of guilt and worthlessness as a result. At its worst, you may feel trapped and severely depressed and think the world would be better off without you. (If your depression gets to this point, you should seek professional help immediately.)

Anger. At first, your anger may show up as interpersonal tension and general irritability. In the latter stages of burnout, this may manifest into angry outbursts and serious arguments at home and at work. (If your anger gets to the point where it turns to thoughts or acts of violence toward family or coworkers, seek immediate professional assistance.)

Burnout doesn't normally just go away on its own so it's worth consulting a mental health professional.

As noted in Chapter 7 "Identity," the impact of racism and other forms of discrimination set up some employees for a higher risk of burnout. Dealing with any form of ongoing exclusion or disadvantage takes a mental and emotional toll, and theoretically predisposes you to burnout.

AVOIDING BURNOUT

Just like you would prepare for an outing in the scorching heat with a generous layer of sunscreen, wide-brimmed hats, and plenty of water, similarly, to avoid burnout you need to identify the risks and then consider these preventive actions.

Plan ahead. Take the time to sort out your calendar in advance so that you can schedule your vacation(s)/staycation(s), book your children's activities, and also to ensure you don't accidentally over-book yourself.

Learn how to say no. This applies to both professional and social demands. If you can't juggle two expectations that will occur at the same time (or too close together), try being honest. It's amazing how others respond when you are forthright about your limits. Note – you can go back to Chapter 5 on boundaries if you skipped ahead and missed it.

To Don't List. Eliminate some stressors by creating a weekly to-don't list of tasks. Evaluate each bullet point on your to-do list by asking:

- Is there someone to whom I can delegate this?
- Can this task wait until another time without creating any problems?
- Can this assignment be altered to make it simpler or less time-consuming?

These simple questions will help you to prioritize your workload while also de-cluttering your obligations.

Stay Healthy. Maintaining a routine of good nutrition, plenty of sleep and exercise can go a long way. This will help to boost your immune system and energy levels to deal with additional activities and work and improve your overall mood so that you can enjoy the summer.

Create some "unavailable hours" for yourself and stick to them. We're all human so there are times when we'll procrastinate, or our work will take longer than we expected. This means that sometimes we'll need to work late even after putting in a full day. To prevent this from becoming a habit, one strategy is to have a set time every day where we give ourselves some time to relax without being beholden to technology or social media. This could mean putting our phone in "do not disturb mode" or not responding to emails until after your morning meditation or coffee. There's something to be said for having some time every day when we don't worry about what other people want from us and we just catch our breath a little.

WORKAHOLISM

Related to the topic of burnout is the concept of workaholism. Research shows a significant positive relationship between workaholism and burnout (e.g., Cheung et al., 2018[1]). They found that workaholism predicted two aspects of job burnout – emotional exhaustion and depersonalization, which they define as negative and detached responses/behavior. I've worked with many clients who have wondered whether they were already a workaholic or if they were becoming one.

These days, many people work all kinds of hours, including some evenings and weekends. Does this mean that they are workaholics? The short answer is no. Some people work long hard hours because they love their work, so they spend a long time enjoying what they're doing. In other situations, the person feels obligated to work a lot.

Many self-employed people, business owners, and professionals will work a variety of daytime, evening, and weekend hours. I know a lawyer who often works very early in the morning from 4 am to 6 am on certain tasks. In exchange for late-night, weekend, and early morning hours, these people may take Fridays off to play golf or tennis, schedule hair or nail appointments during the workday, or take time off when things are slower/quieter to keep things in balance.

To be classified as a "workaholic," a person has to have a very strong need for work which has become so excessive that it has a negative impact on their health and well-being, relationships, and social functioning.

The distinction between work behaviors (that is, working long hours) and a person's mentality around work (i.e., a compulsion to work, or what we call workaholism) is important. Simply working long hours isn't associated with poor health. In contrast, workaholism is linked to more health-related complaints, sleep disturbances, emotional exhaustion, cynicism, and depression. To be even more specific, health and well-being among workaholics, regardless of how much they love their job, can be impaired.

Workaholism is due to a real or perceived obligation to work. This is an especially important concept since so many people started working from home during the pandemic. I'd argue that we can feel overworked and/or burned out because of how we think and/or feel about our work … whether our perceptions are accurate or not.

Sometimes we can put extra or unnecessary pressure on ourselves to work. This pressure could be based on a desire to provide a certain lifestyle for ourselves or our loved ones, due to our ambition, perfectionism/pride, etc. Other times, we are taking on additional work because of our circumstances. It could be a busy period in our organization, there are deadlines to meet, we're understaffed, etc.

Unfortunately, I've known too many people who are overworked to the point of workaholism and/or burnout as a result of an overly demanding or toxic workplace. For instance, there are times when someone is in an unreasonably challenging and high-stakes position that requires an extraordinary ongoing effort with little chance of success. Or, there are times when an employee is the victim of a bully boss who has put them on a contrived performance management regime where they're forced to participate in punitive and (sometimes) humiliating additional scrutiny and burdensome administrative tasks.

In these situations, the employee's work performance isn't problematic. Rather, their employer/superior is abusing their power to mistreat the employee in a way that has the appearance of being warranted and based on the employee's poor work. This is different from legitimate performance management where someone's work is substandard, and improvement is important and necessary.

NOTE

1 Cheung, F., Tang, C., Lim, M., & Koh, J. M. (2018). Workaholism on job burnout: A comparison between American and Chinese employees. *Frontiers in Psychology*, *9*, 2546. www.ncbi.nlm.nih.gov/pmc/articles/PMC6298417/

CHAPTER 11

When It's Time to Change Jobs

Whether things have gone well, or you've bounced back from very challenging or even toxic workplace situations, sometimes it's worthwhile to consider changing jobs. In this chapter, I draw heavily on the experiences of countless clients to consolidate ideas and considerations to bear in mind when contemplating a job change.

Sometimes, even after successfully weaving around professional minefields, you may decide that a particular job has run its course. Maybe you know that you have outgrown your role or organization. Maybe you have been through a lot in that work environment, and you want a fresh start somewhere, without the negative memories or baggage.

There are many times when I have helped clients find a new form of employment so that they can make better use of their professional potential and/or move to an organization that has a much more welcoming and better climate. During these moments, my triple roles as an executive coach, career coach, and HR consultant have been super relevant. As an executive coach, I have intimate knowledge about leadership behaviors and where leaders may stumble. As a career coach, I have a depth of insights regarding current and emerging roles across a range of industries. Finally, as an HR consultant who has created numerous hiring and promotion processes, and career development programs (e.g., succession planning and mentorship programs) for employers, I can anticipate much of what my clients will face going forward. Since the stakes are often high for my clients who have high incomes and ongoing financial obligations, I rely on all of my past experiences when helping them make a transition into a new role – while minimizing potential risks.

 DOI: 10.4324/9781003328988-12

HIDDEN JOB OPPORTUNITIES

There are numerous ways to get access to new job opportunities. This normally involves some tweaks to clients' natural job search process. When my clients are still employed, I encourage them to build and maintain professional relationships since the people to whom they are connected may lead them to the 48% of work-related opportunities that are never advertised. In my experience, many of the higher-quality jobs are discussed informally between friends and associates before they are officially posted publicly – or instead of ever posting them. When you are in the loop and hear about these opportunities via word of mouth through friends, colleagues, and loose connections/acquaintances, it is easier to get an introduction to someone who is responsible for filling the role. That is so much better than applying online and taking your chances with a screening process that's fueled by artificial intelligence or even random selection (whereby software will confirm the presence of basic criteria but then randomly select people who will move on in the hiring process).

When you are invited to apply for jobs through referrals from people who work in organizations with vacant positions, the process is much less competitive. Job openings can be promoted/shared via email, phone, and in-person discussion but often it also includes social media. Countless opportunities are shared via LinkedIn and Facebook, and, to a lesser extent, Instagram and Twitter. This can be semi-public where the opportunity is posted as a status update. But there are times when the opportunity is only quietly shared via the direct message feature. When you are well connected because of your wide and open network, your social media feeds are more likely to include some of these opportunities. When you are poorly connected, you miss opportunities because the people who are in the know do not have your email address or phone number and are not connected to you on social media. So, I like to remember the expression, "it's not only what you know but who you know … and who knows you."

When trying to build out a better professional network, consider these two principles: The know, like, and trust rule and the networking continuum.

KNOW, LIKE, AND TRUST FACTOR

The know, like, and trust rule is simple and says that people do business with, and like to work with, people they know, like, and trust. The "know factor" includes what people know about you (i.e., your work-related background and your interests), the organizations you belong to or support, and other things that are learnable through your LinkedIn profile. These are also the types of things that are knowable via a person's "About" page if they have a website.

The "like factor" is also straightforward: People like other people who are helpful, kind, and not pushy ... Just like most moms and kindergarten teachers taught us.

The "trust factor" is also simple, but it has two parts. The first part is that people trust that you are competent, or if appropriate, an expert. This could include testimonials on your website or public review page and letters of recommendation. This also includes having endorsements and other people vouching for you by describing your skills, expertise, abilities. This can even include scholarships and/or awards. The second part of the Trust Factor is confidence that you will behave decently. This comes from experiences with you that demonstrate that you are consistently helpful, reasonable, and cooperative and recommendations from others describing your positive attitude.

It is worth noting that trust and your reputation can be damaged very quickly. This is why I recommend that if you're active online, your online persona should be consistent with the real you. When people meet or interact with you in person or by video, the "you" that they encounter should be similar to the "you" that you've shared on social media, etc. When there's a disconnect between your online and in-real-life personas, it will be hard for people to know which "you" is real … and this will undermine any trust that you may have established up until that point.

THE NETWORKING CONTINUUM

Years ago, while preparing to deliver a (paid) talk, I came across a business development and networking continuum[1] and process that Dr. Ivan Misner, Founder of Business Network International (BNI), author, and keynote speaker has described in some of his books and videos. It spells out a three-step process that one can use as a guide when building a network. The first step is visibility, people get to know who you are and what you do. The second step is credibility, people know who you are and what you do – and that you're good at it. The final step is profitability, people know who you are and what you do and that you're good at it and they're willing to vouch for you by offering introductions, testimonials, or referrals … on an ongoing basis. In the context of employment, this means that others are confident in suggesting you as a candidate for various opportunities including higher quality files, projects, and promotions.

So, following the logic, your goal should be to gain visibility with people. Then, perform activities that will help you build trust and credibility with them. Finally, through time and the strengthening of that relationship, they will most likely vouch for you in the final profitability stage.

TYPES OF JOBS TO LOOK FOR

When possible and appropriate, I use psychometric testing (as described in Chapter 1) in addition to creative thinking when helping clients become unstuck and identify new job options. If you're going through the exercise of identifying new or different work opportunities, it's wise to identify and think about your transferrable skills, namely, any skills you have mastered that are useful to employers across various jobs and industries. For example, event planners have excellent organizational skills and often consider an event to be a project. If an event planner was pivoting, they might do well if they focus on their exceptional planning and organizing skills, and their project management skills that will be relevant in other roles. So, the takeaway is to identify other contexts where your skills and experience could be valuable. One caveat is that it's worth trying to focus on roles in industries that are growing (e.g., biotech, green industries, machine learning, artificial intelligence, and any companies that are involved in those supply chains). The pandemic also highlighted the value of the arts which add so much value and pleasure to our lives. Industries and fields that are growing should have more opportunities. In contrast, work roles that are associated with heavy pollution or outdated technologies (e.g., landlines, fax, etc.) are probably worth avoiding.

There have been times when excellent employees were overlooked despite their valuable contributions to the success of their organization. Sadly, these "doers" were taken for granted rather than celebrated and respected. If this is how your career has gone so far, there is plenty of hope. One upside is that you may have developed a depth and range of experience that is beyond your peers who have worked just as long because you have been working so much harder. Another advantage is that if you can find a role where you will be rewarded with bonuses or other forms of advancement for working hard and delivering results, it makes sense to pursue those opportunities. Roles including sales, business development, law, consulting, etc. where performance is easy to demonstrate and measure – and tied to compensation, status, and bonuses – may be especially relevant and appealing for many reasons.

SKILLS AND/OR TRAINING

I'm often asked if certain types of skills or training are worth pursuing. Now more than ever, when a client already has a post-secondary degree or diploma, it's rare that I'll suggest that they earn another. In my experience, there are too many people with advanced degrees who are underemployed, so I do not always see training and education as the differentiator.

Plus, the financial and opportunity costs of additional training and education can be hard to justify. Normally, I like my clients to try to identify the gaps between their current skills and education versus the skills and education required by a role that they hope to have in the future. Once the gap is clear, it is possible to reverse engineer or fill in the gaps by acquiring the skills that they need to become competitive for the type of role that they are seeking.

One question I often ask my clients is "are your skills up-to-date and current?" When new people start to work at your organization, do they have the same skills and experience that you have? If they have different or superior training than you have, then it is worth reflecting on that and trying to find ways to ensure that your skills remain current and relevant.

Another question that I ask my clients is "what's the last thing you learned/taught yourself?" If they feel stumped or realize that they are not learning anything by reading, listening, or watching something that supports their career development, I make some suggestions. I normally prioritize fast, free, and lower-cost training and development options (e.g., Coursera, EdX, Udemy, Ivy League massive open online courses (MOOCs), reading, or listening to books, watching videos/documentaries, podcasts, etc.).

MULTIPLE STREAMS OF INCOME

Sometimes, because of necessity, we cannot rely on one job. It could be that there are not enough hours or enough pay associated with the one role when compared to your financial obligations. My rationale for being open to more than one stream of income is that, when you have multiple streams, it is not likely that all of them will be dormant or slow at the same time. Since I work mainly with professionals, I suggest that they choose potential income streams based on their thought leadership. This involves identifying the core skills possessed by the thought leaders and influencers in your industry and developing similar skills. Also, develop unique adjacent skills not possessed by many of the current leaders in your space. For instance, someone who has strengths in writing could also develop additional streams of income from public speaking and/or training. In terms of the order, I think it is best to start one income source at a time. Specifically, this would mean focusing on one stream until it generates income, then adding another. The best income sources are those that can exist independently of each other; if one goes bust, it won't damage the others. In addition, when possible, make your income sources interdependent; if one succeeds, it will increase the success of others.

If you're considering some freelance or contract work that's aligned with your current field, do make sure that you check your current contract or the letter of offer that you signed to confirm that you can do some outside work. There may be non-compete clauses or other wording that prevents you from pursuing certain options.

ENTREPRENEURSHIP

While it is not for everybody, entrepreneurship and self-employment are often viable alternatives. These options can be extremely versatile and can have many spinoff benefits. For people who are very experienced in fields where there is a demand for their insights and services as a consultant or contractor, this is a natural option after a certain point in one's career.

In the United States, BIPOC employees, especially Black women are turning to entrepreneurship[2] to avoid being mistreated, underpaid, and overlooked in the workplace, as reported by Fortune in 2015,[3] Forbes in 2018,[4] and Entrepreneur in 2019. Similar patterns have been seen among Black Canadian women[5] and reported in 2021. On many occasions, I have seen first-hand how entrepreneurship has been used to offset underemployment, and to escape a work-place where someone is experiencing racial discrimination, harassment, or bullying. Of course, entrepreneurship or self-employment is also an option for certain people following a termination, downsizing, or retirement.

At a minimum, creating a "side hustle" can be a great way to generate additional income and develop valuable skills that you may be denied at your day job when you've been passed over for a promotion at work.

I know that there are plenty of business coaches out there that do not believe in "side hustles" or part-time businesses. They believe that "real" businesses require that the owner is "all in" and must succeed in order to survive because there's no base salary to rely on. People who share this perspective will argue that part-time businesses are not "real" businesses and there's just not enough time available during evenings and weekends to become successful. I do not share the traditional business coach perspective; I acknowledge the numerous benefits of a side hustle.

Work/Organizational Psychologist Dr. Adam Grant has shared some insights based on applied research in his book called *Originals*.[6] He notes that side hustles allow people to be more innovative and take bigger calculated risks because they are not counting on the business to cover their living expenses. He argues that the relative security of knowing you have a good day job can provide the peace of mind that frees you for innovation. More importantly, if you start a side hustle, you are 33% less likely to fail than if you start full-time from day one. Richard Branson, a famous entrepreneur is also a fan of the side hustle. His company Virgin started as a side hustle and he acknowledges that all the Virgin businesses started while they were working on something else.

New technology has made self-employment easier than ever before – and changes in the economy make entrepreneurship almost a necessity. A 2017 survey conducted by Bankrate[7] reports that 44 million Americans have part-time businesses or "side hustles." In 2021, Startup Canada[8] reported that we have a community of 3.5 million entrepreneurs in Canada, and some portion of those are part-time businesses.

Basically, what we are seeing is an updated version of moonlighting. In the past, moonlighting was usually a second job that someone went to outside of their usual full-time work hours. The current version is different because the "side hustle" is often some form of small business that's done in addition to one's full-time job – often from home. Sometimes, the part-time entrepreneur is creating and selling products (e.g., fancy cakes, hot sauce, or jewelry), other times, the side hustle is a service (e.g., building and maintaining websites, managing social media accounts, or bookkeeping). The Internet has lowered the barrier to entry for many types of businesses. Further, for some digital businesses, the owner can continue to earn money while they are simultaneously working elsewhere and drawing an income.

The success and viability of these side hustles varies. Some remain small and generate extra income for their owners while others become lucrative and grow large enough in scale so that the owner can focus on it full time.

I can't argue against Grant or Branson – obviously, their perspectives have merit. I, will, however, also highlight some additional benefits of entrepreneurship.

BUILDING SKILLS OUTSIDE OF WORK

Sometimes our full-time jobs help us to pay our bills, but they don't provide opportunities to develop new skills or abilities. Side hustles can allow us to use and demonstrate leadership, engage in more strategic work, more creative work, public speaking, or other domains. Once skills and abilities have been honed, it is for you, the owner of those skills to determine where and when to use them. It could lay the foundation for a promotion, full-time business, a career change, or demonstrating experience in a new country or industry.

BUILT-IN RESILIENCE

In my line of work, I've seen good people lose their jobs because of restructuring, downsizing, ageism, scapegoating, the glass cliff, etc. Depending on the client's age and skill set, self-employment may be a very wise choice. In certain fields, having a modest side hustle in place creates a natural backup plan so that if things ever take a dramatic turn for the worse at work, you have got something that you can build from.

A REMEDY FOR UNDEREMPLOYMENT

There are times when we are working in a role that we're overqualified for. When this happens, and someone has been pigeon-holed into a limited role, one way to break free of this is to find concrete and measurable ways to demonstrate one's value in other roles. Excellent metrics to substantiate your accomplishments/value include revenue generated and testimonials – these are natural by-products of a viable side hustle. Most job postings will allow you to demonstrate why you are qualified for the role in your cover letter and resume and you can use your side hustle in both documents when it suits you.

A CAREER AFTER RETIREMENT

Some employees realize that, after a long career, they will earn almost as much money working full time as they will if they retire and start to live off their pension (especially once taxes are factored in). If you're in this fortunate position to be able to retire and pursue some type of part-time consulting or another role, the side hustle is probably just the right pace and a wonderful way to remain adequately engaged during your semi-retirement.

BUILDING EQUITY IN YOUR OWN LIVELIHOOD

I've come to appreciate that you don't usually build up "equity" as an employee the same way that you build equity as a business owner or self-employed person. Your "value" as an employee does not necessarily increase over time, it is pretty flat. You do, however, develop transferable skills, and work experience, and (hopefully) grow a network as you progress in your career. On the flip side, as a self-employed person or business owner, one can, and usually does, build equity in something that you have control over.

SELF-EMPLOYMENT: A REALITY CHECK

Once you've considered some of the important preliminaries – what you want to do and what you'd be good at – it's important that you take a sober look at your strengths and weaknesses and confirm you're right for entrepreneurship. I often tell clients, *"just because you can do something doesn't mean that you should do it."* When you are out on your own as an entrepreneur, your personality traits, strengths, and weaknesses will be magnified. You will need to find ways to consistently compensate for your weaknesses and make great use of your strengths.

Ideally, you'll have a chance to plan things out and do some thorough research while you still have a steady pay cheque. Also, you can ease into your business and learn as you go with a side hustle.

Do your due diligence. Research, research, research. Get out and talk to entrepreneurs. Go to business networking meetings and events. Find out what it's *really* like to be your own boss. For example, if you've been an employee for some years, you've probably never approached a lender to ask for a small business loan. When Jane Smith (a former client) left the federal government to open her own clothing shop, she says she experienced a "rude awakening."

For one thing, once she wasn't a civil servant, the financial institution that held her mortgage was a lot less friendly. "Once I became self-employed, they had very little time for me. I couldn't get a small business loan or line of credit because my business was too new. I couldn't even get an overdraft for my business account."

As for the "freedom" aspect of being your own boss? Jane learned the hard way that self-employment should not be confused with freedom. "I thought I was going to set my own hours and do things my way. It turned out that I worked longer hours than I ever did before, and I had more bosses than ever. Your customers become your bosses. I ended up with hundreds of bosses to please."

Although entrepreneurship has grown in popularity (possibly as a necessity), it's not a great option for everyone – regardless of the nature of the enterprise. So, whenever I know that someone is contemplating making the transition from employee to a full-time entrepreneur who will depend on the income they can generate, I want them to approach it with their eyes wide open and with plenty of self-awareness. That way, before they take the leap, they will be better prepared.

CAREER CHANGE CAN BE RISKY

In part, this final chapter was inspired by the common question asked by people who are earning a high income when their career gets derailed by a downsizing, merger, acquisition, or other situation that triggers their job loss. Usually, when someone is accustomed to earning a lot of money as an employee, they are reluctant to consider self-employment or entrepreneurship. This is understandable, especially since the experience of job loss for high-earning high performers is extremely disorienting. It is only natural to make sure that if you pivot from one job to another, you remain on some familiar terrain rather than going way out on a limb and trying self-employment. The problem is that most higher paying jobs are less common than similar jobs that pay significantly less. Anecdotally, I've learned that for every extra $10K in annual income, you need to spend an extra month on your job search. In other words, if you plan to earn $150K, it may take you the better part of a year to find a position in your field that pays that much. This begs the question, is it better to try to create something of your own instead of waiting for the next perfect job? Which option is riskier?

Typically, when I broach the idea of self-employment or propose buying a modest franchise, most of my clients do not even want to contemplate it. They have grown accustomed to being valued employees receiving a steady paycheck. Also, they feel more secure when they feel like they are being taken care of by their firm or organization – and there's nothing wrong with that. For good reason, being a business owner or self-employed is perceived as time-consuming and high-risk. Many of my clients want to pursue something that they perceive as safer and will allow them to maintain their lifestyle while meeting their established financial obligations. Those are all realistic (and desirable) concepts to be mindful of. But what if I told you that it could be even riskier to go from one high-paying job to another when you're well into your 40s or 50s?

For many knowledge workers and professionals, as they progress in their careers, their income increases along with their expertise and work experience. This means they become more expensive to their employers. So, by the time a professional enters their late 40s or 50s, they are usually hitting their peak income-earning years.

I have had the privilege of working with high-earning clients who were in their 40s and 50s while they were at a crossroads in their career. I consider this to be an exciting but also a challenging task because often these people are well qualified in their professions and are also accustomed to excellent earnings. This means that the stakes are very high – they can't afford to go from a solid high salary to a considerably lower income because of a misstep or bad decision.

In these clients' cases, something dramatic happened in their workplace. Sometimes it was an unexpected merger and, consequently, their role became redundant. Other times, upper management chose to replace them with someone "fresher" and more "vibrant" (basically coded language for younger) who would willingly work for less money, despite it being glaringly obvious the new employee didn't have the same level of expertise or work experience. In all these situations, my more mature clients were faced with the stressful choice between trying to find another high-paying job or figuring out a way to become their own boss. Unfortunately, both options are associated with major risks.

Most organizations find these hard-working, talented employees valuable to a certain point, but sometimes, in the private sector, they become too expensive to retain. To cope, the business may pay those expensive, top-earning workers a fair severance and then hire someone less experienced who is prepared to work the same or even more hours for much less money. It's a budgeting exercise. The counterintuitive reality is that as one's income rises, it can become increasingly risky to be an employee in the private sector where profit is the main motive. This is perhaps less of a concern in the public sector (e.g., municipal, state/provincial, and federal government, or government-funded elementary or secondary schools, etc.) and in non-profit organizations.

In contrast, over time, once a business owner or self-employed person is established and has a good business model, an adequate source of ongoing referrals, effective marketing, etc. then their risks decrease over time. I appreciate that not all skills and experience lend themselves to self-employment or entrepreneurship but, when they do, there's no denying the upside.

NOTES

1 Misner, I. (2018, March 15). *The three phases of networking: The VCP process®*. Dr. Ivan Misner. https://ivanmisner.com/three-phases-networking-vcp-process/
2 Greenwood, M. (2019, April 9). Black female founders face constant rejection. They're thriving anyway. *Entrepreneur*. www.entrepreneur.com/article/331239
3 Haimerl, A. (2015, June 29). *The fastest-growing group of entrepreneurs in America*. Fortune. https://fortune.com/2015/06/29/black-women-entrepreneurs/
4 Hannon, K. (2018, September 9). *Black women entrepreneurs: The good and not-so-good news*. Forbes. www.forbes.com/sites/nextavenue/2018/09/09/black-women-entrepreneurs-the-good-and-not-so-good-news/?sh=525c8fd66ffe
5 Black Business and Professional Association (BBPA). (2021, April 15). *Canada's largest study of black women entrepreneurs shows significant challenges but also resilience and optimism*. Cision Canada. www.newswire.ca/news-releases/canada-s-largest-study-of-black-women-entrepreneurs-shows-significant-challenges-but-also-resilience-and-optimism-830157113.html

6 Grant, A. (2016). *Originals: How non-conformists move the world.* Viking. https://adamgrant.net/book/originals/

7 Berger, S. (2017, July 12). *Side Hustle Nation: Millennials are making major money with side gigs.* Bankrate. www.bankrate.com/personal-finance/smart-money/side-hustles-survey/

8 Dojchinovska, A. (2021, September 13). 21 groundbreaking Canadian entrepreneur statistics for 2021. *Reviewlution.* Retrieved from https://reviewlution.ca/resources/entrepreneur-statistics/#:~:text=There%20are%20around%203.5%20million, entrepreneurs%20have%20a%20university%20degree

Conclusion

For most people, work is more than just a way to earn a living. Being able to meet our financial obligations and take care of ourselves and our loved ones is important. But how we feel about ourselves also matters. What we think about ourselves is tied to our mindset, and our mindset has an impact on our performance and our success at work. Even under straightforward circumstances, our self-perception and well-being can be skewed and damaged. When our careers and livelihoods go sideways or downward, so much is at stake. During times of work-related crisis, not everyone has a deep network of experienced advisors, mentors, or coaches who can help them sort things out when these inevitable setbacks occur. My sincere hope is that this book will be a trusted resource for those occasions.

The modern workplace has become complicated. It is increasingly rare to find a job right after graduation and work in one organization throughout your career. This means that people need to be more intentional about developing their careers as they move from organization to organization. Following college or university, many graduates have a harder time finding a secure job that pays enough for them to build a comfortable life while also paying off student loans. For past generations, a solid education almost guaranteed a good livelihood. In some ways, the gig economy is booming, but not all gigs pay enough for freelancers to feel confident about their finances. Even for people who have stable employment, factors such as underemployment, impostor syndrome, and the challenges associated with bullying, harassment, and discrimination are profound and difficult to contend with. The pandemic created a massive, instant, and collective organizational change that brought work into many homes. Now more than ever, navigating professional boundaries that have literally merged into our homes is essential. In some cases, this shift was a partial escape from toxic workplaces, but for others, not so much. These factors can make the modern workplace more difficult to navigate.

Dealing with the integration and inclusion of numerous identities and perspectives in an equitable manner can be harder for leaders and employees than it looks. Although it should simply come down to having employees contribute their skills and abilities, the workplace is a microcosm of our larger societies. This means that hidden and less hidden biases, systems, and forms of oppression, do not wait politely outside the doors of our workplaces. It is no wonder that diversity and true equity, inclusion, and belonging have proven to be illusive.

Although often discussed in whispered tones rather than out in the open, burnout, and problematic or toxic workplace behaviors like harassment, bullying, and discrimination are common. This is a lot – both for employees and leaders. I wrote this book so that anyone who finds themselves dealing with any of these common work-related career derailers has somewhere to turn – even if they do not have access to their own private career coach or executive coach. This book should also be a solid resource for friends, allies, and other supporters of people who are experiencing these setbacks. Many employees approach their clinical psychologists, psychotherapists, and social workers to help support their mental health and wellness during challenging times. This book will also arm these mental health service providers and researchers with an insider perspective on the modern workplace.

In 2012, when I was starting I/O Advisory Services, I was explaining my vision to Derek, a childhood friend of my brother. Derek is a renaissance man: Painter, author, bonsai enthusiast, interior designer, sculptor, and welder. Despite his tremendous gifts, he had experienced several career setbacks due to bad fortune rather than a lack of planning or effort. It was Derek who reminded me of the resilience of ferns and how that could be a good metaphor for my business. Ultimately, the conversations that we had led to my tagline: Building Resilient Careers and Organizations. The challenges that I had faced were different from his, but the notion of supporting others as they built resilience was exactly what I wanted to inspire and guide my work. This tagline has been my compass from day one.

As I sign off on this book, I am reminded of a quote that is often misattributed to C.S. Lewis. "Hardships often prepare ordinary people for an extraordinary destiny." In many respects, that is how I see my clients. They are ordinary in the sense that they are not usually famous but, with the right support at the right time, so many of them are now on track to accomplish the extraordinary. I wish the same for you. Aim high.

References/Further Reading

American Addiction Centers. (2022, March 11). Drug & substance abuse addiction statistics. American Addiction Centers. https://americanaddictioncenters.org/rehab-guide/addiction-statistics

Babiak, P., & Hare, R. D. (2006). *Snakes in suits: When psychopaths go to work*. Regan Books/Harper Collins. www.harpercollins.com/products/snakes-in-suits-paul-babiakrobert-d-hare?variant=39689396617250

Berger, S. (2017, July 12). *Side hustle nation: Millennials are making major money with side gigs*. Bankrate. www.bankrate.com/personal-finance/smart-money/side-hustles-survey/

Black Business and Professional Association (BBPA). (2021, April 15). *Canada's largest study of black women entrepreneurs shows significant challenges but also resilience and optimism*. Cision Canada. www.newswire.ca/news-releases/canada-s-largest-study-of-black-women-entrepreneurs-shows-significant-challenges-but-also-resilience-and-optimism-830157113.html

Broecke, S., Singh, S., & Swaim, P. (2016, June). The state of the North American labour market. OECD. www.oecd.org/unitedstates/The-state-of-the-north-american-labour-market-june-2016.pdf

Brown, J. (2016). *Inclusion: Diversity, the new workplace & the will to change*. Advantage Media Group. https://jenniferbrownspeaks.com/jbs-book-inclusion

Bureau of Labor Statistics, and the Center for American Progress. (2020, July). *The high cost of a toxic workplace culture: How culture impacts the workforce – and the bottom line*. SHRM. https://pmq.shrm.org/wp-content/uploads/2020/07/SHRM-Culture-Report_2019-1.pdf

Canadian Charter of Rights and Freedoms, s 15, Part I of the Constitution Act, 1982, being Schedule B to the Canada Act 1982 (UK), 1982, c11.

Cheung, F., Tang, C., Lim, M., & Koh, J. M. (2018). Workaholism on job burnout: A comparison between American and Chinese employees. *Frontiers in Psychology*, 9, 2546. https://doi.org/10.3389/fpsyg.2018.02546

Danielle, B. (2015, May 12). Michelle Obama's "twice as good" speech doesn't cut it with most African Americans. *The Guardian.* www.theguardian.com/commentisfree/2015/may/12/michelle-obama-twice-as-good-african-americans-black-people

DeAngelis, T. (2019, February). The legacy of trauma. *Monitor on Psychology, 50*(2). www.apa.org/monitor/2019/02/legacy-trauma

Deschamps, T. (2019, July 24). Canadian people of colour carry an "emotional tax" at work. *The Hamilton Spectator.* www.thespec.com/business/2019/07/24/canadian-people-of-colour-carry-an-emotional-tax-at-work.html

Dojchinovska, A. (2021, September 13). 21 groundbreaking Canadian entrepreneur statistics for 2021. *Reviewlution.* https://reviewlution.ca/resources/entrepreneur-statistics/#:~:text=There%20are%20around%203.5%20million,entrepreneurs%20have%20a%20university%20degree

Dweck, C. (2015). Carol Dweck revisits the "growth mindset." *Education Week.* www.edweek.org/ew/articles/2015/09/23/carol-dweck-revisits-the-growth-mindset.html?cmp=cpc-goog-ew-growth+mindset&ccid=growth+mindset&ccag=growth+mindset&cckw=%2Bgrowth%20%2Bmindset&cccv=content+ad&gclid=Cj0KEQiAnvfDBRCXrabLl6-6t-0BEiQAW4SRUM7nekFnoTxc675q-BMSJycFgwERohguZWVmNDcSUg5gaAk3I8P8HAQ

Gateway Foundation. (n.d.). The effects of alcohol abuse & addiction. Gateway Foundation. www.gatewayfoundation.org/about-gateway-foundation/faqs/effects-of-alcohol-addiction/

Goffman, E. (1963). *Stigma: Notes on the management of spoiled identity.* Simon & Schuster, p. 102.

Grant, A., (Host), (2018, April). When work takes over your life (Season 1, Episode 8) [Audio podcast episode]. In *Worklife with Adam Grant.* Ted Audio Collective. https://podcasts.apple.com/us/podcast/the-office-without-a-holes/id1346314086?i=1000433927551

Grant, A., (Host), (2019, April 9). The office without A**holes (Season 2, Episode 5) [Audio podcast episode]. In *Worklife with Adam Grant.* Ted Audio Collective. https://podcasts.apple.com/us/podcast/the-office-without-a-holes/id1346314086?i=1000433927551

Grant, A. (2016). *Originals: How non-conformists move the world.* Viking. https://adamgrant.net/book/originals/

Greenwood, M. (2019, April 9). Black female founders face constant rejection. They're thriving anyway. *Entrepreneur.* www.entrepreneur.com/article/331239

Haimerl, A. (2015, June 29). *The fastest-growing group of entrepreneurs in America.* Fortune. https://fortune.com/2015/06/29/black-women-entrepreneurs/

Hannon, K. (2018, September 9). *Black women entrepreneurs: The good and not-so-good news.* Forbes. www.forbes.com/sites/nextavenue/2018/09/09/black-women-entrepreneurs-the-good-and-not-so-good-news/?sh=525c8fd66ffe

Harvey, C. (2018). When queen bees attack women stop advancing: Recognising and addressing female bullying in the workplace. *Development and Learning in Organizations, 32*(5), 1–4. https://doi.org/10.1108/DLO-04-2018-0048

Hirsch, L. (2021, January 23). The business case for boardroom diversity. *The New York Times.* www.nytimes.com/section/todayspaper

Huang, J., Krivkovich, A., Starikova, I., Yea, L., & Zanoschi, D. (2019, October). Women in the workplace 2019. McKinsey. www.mckinsey.com/~/media/McKinsey/Featured%20Insights/Gender%20Equality/Women%20in%20the%20Workplace%202019/Women-in-the-workplace-2019.ashx

Isaacson, W. (2011). *Steve Jobs.* Simon & Schuster. www.simonandschuster.com/books/Steve-Jobs/Walter-Isaacson/9781982176860

Isidore, C. (2020, December 2). *Nasdaq to corporate America: Make your boards more diverse or get out.* CNN. Retrieved May 22 2022 from www.cnn.com/2020/12/01/investing/nasdaq-rule-board-of-directors-diversity/index.html

Jana, T. (2021, September 24). How to lose a chief diversity officer in 6 months. *Medium.* https://index.medium.com/how-to-lose-a-chief-diversity-officer-in-6-months-6db0dfba6169

Johnson, M. (n.d.). *Sexual harassment training essential in all States.* Clear Law Institute. https://clearlawinstitute.com/harassment-training-essential-employees-states-not-just-california-supervisors/

Kendi, I. (2019). *How to be an antiracist.* One World.

LeanIn.Org and McKinsey & Company (2020, August 13). *The state of Black Women in corporate America.* Lean In and Mckinsey & Company https://media.sgff.io/sgff_r1eHetbDYb/2020-08-13/1597343917539/Lean_In_-_State_of_Black_Women_in_Corporate_America_Report_1.pdf

Mattice, C. (2020, July 10). *A closer look: Workplace bullying vs. harassment.* Employment Background Investigations. www.ebiinc.com/a-closer-look-workplace-bullying-vs-harassment-workplace-violence/

McCullough, D. G. (2014, August 8). Women CEOS: Why companies in crisis hire minorities – and then fire them. *The Guardian.* www.theguardian.com/sustainable-business/2014/aug/05/fortune-500-companies-crisis-woman-ceo-yahoo-xerox-jc-penny-economy

Misner, I. (2018, March 15). *The three phases of networking: The VCP process®*. Dr. Ivan Misner. https://ivanmisner.com/three-phases-networking-vcp-process/

Pearson, C., Ali, J., & Janz, T. (2015, November 27). *Mental and substance use disorders in Canada (No. 82-624-X)*. Statistics Canada. www150.statcan.gc.ca/n1/pub/82-624-x/2013001/article/11855-eng.htm

Perry, B. D., & Winfrey, O. (2021). *What happened to you?: Conversations on trauma, resilience, and healing*. Flatiron Books.

Posner, C. (2020, December 2). Blog: Nasdaq proposes a "comply or explain" Board diversity mandate. JD Supra. www.jdsupra.com/legalnews/blog-nasdaq-proposes-a-comply-or-29494/

Powers, L. (2015, October 2). Tories pledge new RCMP Tip Line to report forced marriage and other "barbaric practices." CBC News. www.cbc.ca/news/politics/canada-election-2015-barbaric-cultural-practices-law-1.3254118

Queen's Printer for Ontario. (2022, March 2). Preventing workplace violence and workplace harassment. Ontario.ca. www.ontario.ca/page/preventing-workplace-violence-and-workplace-harassment

Racco, M. (2018, August 28). Two-thirds of women say they've been bullied by another woman in the workplace. Global News. https://globalnews.ca/news/4411507/women-workplace-bullying/

Reuters in Toronto. (2022, June 15). Toronto police chief apologizes to people of color over disproportionate use of force. *The Guardian*. www.theguardian.com/world/2022/jun/15/toronto-police-people-of-color-face-disproportionate-use-of-force

Rodriguez, T. (2021, August 5). Covid-19's continuing toll: Increasing alcohol use and liver disease disproportionately affect women. *Psychiatry Advisor*. www.psychiatryadvisor.com/home/topics/addiction/alcohol-related-disorders/covid-19-pandemic-disproportionate-affect-on-women-led-to-increased-alcohol-use/

Rogers, L., & Wilder, K. (2020, June 25). Shift in working-age population relative to older and younger Americans. Census.gov. www.census.gov/library/stories/2020/06/working-age-population-not-keeping-pace-with-growth-in-older-americans.html

Rohrich, Z. (2019, April 1). How Brexit became a "glass cliff" for Theresa May. PBS. www.pbs.org/newshour/world/how-brexit-became-a-glass-cliff-for-theresa-may

Ryan, M. K., & Haslam, S. A. (2005). The glass cliff: Evidence that women are over-represented in precarious leadership positions. *British Journal of Management, 16*(2), 81–90. https://doi.org/10.1111/j.1467-8551.2005.00433.x

Smith, C., & Yoshino, K. (2019). *Uncovering talent a new model of inclusion*. Deloitte. www2.deloitte.com/content/dam/Deloitte/us/Documents/about-deloitte/us-about-deloitte-uncovering-talent-a-new-model-of-inclusion.pdf

Sneader, K., & Yee, L. (2019, January). One is the loneliest number. *McKinsey Quarterly*. www.mckinsey.com/featured-insights/gender-equality/one-is-the-loneliest-number

Snee, T. (2020, October 13). Bored at work: Workers who feel overqualified are more likely to look for new jobs. Tippie College of Business. https://tippie.uiowa.edu/news/bored-work-workers-who-feel-overqualified-are-more-likely-look-new-jobs

Statista Research Department. (2021, March 31). *United States: Victims of sexual harassment in 2017, by gender*. [Data set]. Statista. www.statista.com/statistics/787997/share-of-americans-who-have-been-victims-of-sexual-harassment-gender/

Stout, M. (2005). *The sociopath next door: The ruthless versus the rest of us*. Broadway Books. www.penguinrandomhouse.ca/books/174276/the-sociopath-next-door-by-martha-stout-phd/9780767915823/excerpt

Sull, D., Sull, C., & Zweig, B. (2022, January 11). Toxic culture is driving the great resignation. *MIT Sloan Management Review*. https://sloanreview.mit.edu/article/toxic-culture-is-driving-the-great-resignation/#article-authors

Sull, D., Sull, C., Cipolli, W., & Brighenti, C. (2022, March 16). Why every leader needs to worry about toxic culture. *MIT Sloan Management Review*. https://sloanreview.mit.edu/article/why-every-leader-needs-to-worry-about-toxic-culture/

Tong, T. (2019, March 28). The "glass cliff" puts women in power during crisis – often without support. *The World*. www.pri.org/stories/2019-03-28/glass-cliff-puts-women-power-during-crisis-often-without-support

U.S. Department of Health and Human Services. (2015, November 18). *10 percent of US adults have drug use disorder at some point in their lives*. National Institutes of Health. www.nih.gov/news-events/news-releases/10-percent-us-adults-have-drug-use-disorder-some-point-their-lives

Universal Class. (n.d.). *Federal law and workplace harassment*. UniversalClass.com. www.universalclass.com/articles/business/federal-law-and-workplace-harassment.htm#:~:text=The%20primary%20federal%20law%20that,Civil%20Rights%20Act%20of%201964.&text=At%20the%20moment%2C%20it%20formally,the%20exception%20of%20sexual%20orientation

Usher, A. (2018, May 4). *Visible minority numbers rise sharply*. HESA. http://higheredstrategy.com/visible-minority-participation-in-university-studies/

White, M. C. (2014, February 10). 5 signs you're overqualified for your job. *Time*. https://business.time.com/2014/02/10/5-signs-youre-overqualified-for-your-job/.

Zweigenhaft, R., & Dana, C. A. (2020, October 28). Fortune 500 CEOS, 2000–2020: Still male, still white. *The Society Pages*. Retrieved from https://thesocietypages.org/specials/fortune-500-ceos-2000-2020-still-male-still-white/

About the Author

 **Dr. Helen Ofosu** completed her studies at McMaster University and the University of Windsor, Ontario, Canada. In addition to Career and Executive Coaching, her specialties include the assessment and development of leadership skills, inclusive recruitment and selection of staff and executives, and navigating the complex issues of workplace bullying, harassment, diversity, equity, and inclusion.

Dr. Ofosu has over 20 years of experience using Work and Business Psychology in the private sector and the public and non-profit sectors. Before starting I/O Advisory Services[1] in 2012, Dr. Ofosu worked for the Public Service Commission of Canada, the Department of Foreign Affairs and International Trade (now Global Affairs Canada), and the Department of National Defence. She has developed online screening tests, structured interviews, role-plays, and simulations, etc. for evaluating job applicants' skills and behaviors as part of the hiring, development, and promotion process. She continues to do this work in the private, non-profit, and public sectors through her consulting practice. Her work has been recognized with three national awards and it has been used by hiring managers to identify talented job candidates across a range of occupations. She has a unique approach to corporate mentorship to support protégés' career development while also developing leadership skills among the mentors. Since 2012, Dr. Ofosu has worked with clients in Canada, the United States, the United Arab Emirates, South Africa, Ghana, Saudi Arabia, Germany, and elsewhere.

Dr. Ofosu is an Adjunct Professor of Psychology at Carleton University in Ottawa, Canada and in 2021, she was one of five founding officers of a new section of the Canadian Psychological Association (CPA) that is focused on Black Psychology. This is an important step toward improving the representation of Black graduate students, faculty, and practitioners of psychology in Canada.

Born in Toronto, she lives in Ottawa, Canada with her partner Errol and teenage son Kojo.

This is an important step toward improving the representation of Black graduate students, faculty, and practitioners of psychology in Canada.

For more about Dr. Ofosu, visit:

Website:	https://ioadvisory.com/
Facebook page:	www.facebook.com/IOAdvisoryServices
Twitter handle:	@drheleno_ca
LinkedIn:	www.linkedin.com/in/helenofosu
Instagram:	@drheleno_ca

NOTE

1 https://ioadvisory.com/

Index

red flags 21; vague feedback 21;
see also credentials; qualifications;
underemployment or being
overqualified
pseudo-science 11
psychometric testing 5–6, 9–13;
advantages of assessments 10;
"Big Five" tests 9; free or paid-
for tests 11; hiring decisions 11;
leadership assessments 12–13;
as part, not whole, of evaluation
process 11–12; professional
development 12
psychopathy 79–80, 83, 85–87

qualifications 22–25; of author
22–23; being overqualified
see underemployment or being
overqualified; PhD 23, 24;
see also credentials
"Queen Bee Syndrome" 52–55

racial discrimination 111, 168
racism: anti-Black/anti-Indigenous
43–44, 107, 116, 118, 119;
in Canada 43–44, 107, 118;
global culture 109; racialized
immigrants 30; racialized job
candidates and students 19;
racialized leaders 7, 124–126;
systemic 44, 107, 108–109, 121;
in the United States 109–111,
115, 116, 118
RCMP *see* Royal Canadian
Mounted Police (RCMP)
relaxation 159
remote working 140
resignations 51–52
resilience 5, 41, 133, 135; built-in
170–171
Royal Canadian Mounted Police
(RCMP) 118, 122
ruminate 45, 61
Ryan, Michelle 147, 152

scapegoats, dealing with
142, 143–146; counselling/
therapy, considering 145;
getting one's own legal advice

144–145; "intersecting" issues,
seeking nuanced counsel 145;
outplacement/career coaching,
signing up for 145; wrongful
dismissal process, using legal
assistance 145
Securities and Exchange
Commission, US 125–126
segmentors 62–63
self-confidence 48, 73, 145
self-employment 26–27, 30, 160,
175; and deciding to change jobs
169, 172–173; income 35; and
networking 135, 138; risks
173–174; *see also* entrepreneurship
self-awareness 173
sensitivity training 111–112
setbacks *see* challenges and obstacles
sexual harassment 52, 54, 55–59,
145; abuse, women's claims
of 57–58; and bullying 58;
confronting the abuser 58;
see also bullying in workplace;
harassment
"side hustle," creating 133, 169–170
Sigma Beta Phi Sorority, Ottawa 113
Sixteen Personality Factor
Questionnaire (16PF) 11
skills: building outside of work
170; implications of failing to use
18; reframing 26; soft 3; special
49; and/or training 166–167;
utilizing in a new way 35
Snakes in Suits (Babiak and
Hare) 79, 84
Sneader, K. 42–43, 114
Society for Human Resource
Management (SHRM) 87–88
The Society Pages 142
The Sociopath Next Door (Stout) 81
soft skills 3
Starbucks 110–111
Startup Canada 169
Statistica Research Department,
US 56
Statistics Canada 56, 71
STEM (Science, Technology,
Engineering and Mathematics)
42, 116

For Product Safety Concerns and Information please contact our EU
representative GPSR@taylorandfrancis.com
Taylor & Francis Verlag GmbH, Kaufingerstraße 24, 80331 München, Germany

www.ingramcontent.com/pod-product-compliance
Ingram Content Group UK Ltd.
Pitfield, Milton Keynes, MK11 3LW, UK
UKHW021425080625
459435UK00011B/165